ADMIRERER
of
MiKE Dougherty

Discovering Your Language

Discovering Your Language

NEIL POSTMAN · HAROLD MORINE
GRETA MORINE

HOLT, RINEHART AND WINSTON, INC.
NEW YORK

Preface

From the time the authors conceived of this book until the time it was published, three years elapsed. During those years, many devoted and competent people contributed their ideas, time, and skills in an effort to improve the book. None gave more help than Dr. Raymond Sheele, of Hofstra College, and Mr. Howard Damon, of New York University. Their experience, scholarship, and imagination were invaluable to us during all stages of our testing and writing of the materials.

We also owe a considerable debt of gratitude to those teachers of English, who, throwing caution to the winds, were willing to test our material in their classes, and who were frank to tell us what was both right and wrong with the text. They are: Geoffrey Dwyer, Charles Gray, Julio Rodriguez, Arnold Spinner, and Charles Swenson of Brentwood Junior High School, Brentwood, Long Island; Frank Asher, of Memorial Junior High School, Fairlawn, New Jersey; and Miss Moira Devine, of Scarsdale Junior High School, Scarsdale, New York.

Others who helped and encouraged us in various ways are Dr. Bernard Weiss, Curriculum Coordinator, Detroit Public School system; Professor James Gordon, University of Pennsylvania; Professor Priscilla Tyler, Harvard University; and Dr. Eugene Hoyt, Brentwood Junior High School. We wish also to express our gratitude to the New York State Department of Education which encouraged our testing of much of the material contained in the text.

Finally, we would like to thank all of the junior high school students who took part in a three-year educational adventure.

Their warm and intelligent responses have led us to believe that other students will find *Discovering Your Language* interesting and useful.

NEIL POSTMAN

HAROLD MORINE

GRETA MORINE

Contents

Discovering Your Language

PART
I

*Initial
Explorations*

CHAPTER 1

What is language?

In a world of split atoms, man-made moons, and such movies as "I Was a Teen-Age Visitor from Outer Space," our imaginations have to be quite lively in order to keep up with the times. Therefore, it should not be too hard for you to imagine, for a moment, that some creature from Venus has been sent to Earth to observe human beings. Now, imagine further that he has been asked by his leaders to pay close attention to what human beings look like and what kinds of things they do. If our creature made his observations even in a casual way, he would probably notice that human beings look very much alike, but that there are differences in their appearances. He would notice, too, that Earth people wear different kinds

of clothing and that the differences are usually accounted for by the nature of the climate in which people live and the kind of work they do.

Our creature would probably notice other things, too. For example, Earth people usually live in groups which sometimes do not get along very well with one another. They move about on two legs (except for those who use something called an "automobile"). They eat animals, fish, plants and, sometimes, even each other. They spend about a third of their lives in an unconscious condition which they call "sleeping" (although some people seem unconscious even when they are not sleeping). Some of the Earth people keep their younger and more energetic members locked in a building called a "school house" for many hours of each day.

But, perhaps the most obvious feature—and our creature from outer space would surely not fail to observe it— is that human beings are almost constantly making noises at each other. In fact, they stop doing this only when they are sleeping or putting food into their mouths. If our creature were *very* observant (and super-intelligent creatures from outer space always are!), he would notice

5

that these noises differ greatly, depending on whether one is in Tokyo, Japan, or Brentwood, Long Island, or some other remote place on Earth. Assuming that our visitor were especially interested in studying this feature of human behavior, he would discover that there are more than three thousand different sets of noises that Earth people make and that each one of these sets is known as a "language."

Now, imagine that our fictional visitor from outer space has finished his observations of Earth people. He meets his small space ship in some secret place. From here he speeds away to the mother ship, which has been hovering above the Earth's atmosphere waiting for him. (The mother spaceship, meanwhile, has had a terrible time trying to escape being hit by American and Russian rockets headed for the moon.) The mother ship gently picks up the saucer, briefly gives off a greenish-blue glow, and then rockets away at an incredible speed. When our visitor returns to Venus, he makes his official report to his leaders from which they conclude that Earth people are more dangerous to themselves than to Space people. Immediately afterward, he begins writing an article about his adventures. The title of his article is, naturally, "I Visited a Teen-Age Planet." Shortly after it is written, it is published in the Sunday edition of *The Venutian Times*. The article, of course, is too lengthy to be completely reproduced here, but, if your imagination has been stirred, you might like to read part of what our Venutian author wrote about "language" on Earth.

½ ¢ per copy **The Venutian Times**

WEATHER
COOL TODAY
IN 90s
NORMAL TONITE
-20° to -30°

EXTRA!!

EARTHSEER REPORTS

EXCLUSIVE:

Fantastic Manner of Speaking in Noises Found With Inhabitants of Earth Planet!!!!!

"All Earth people speak a *language*. A language is noises. These noises are of various kinds which Earth people usually make by doing things with their throats, tongues, lips, and teeth. Earth babies learn a language by listening to the noises that their parents make, observing the things to which the noises refer, and imitating these noises. It is a very clever procedure.

"Each noise stands for something in a particular language. For example, a person from Oceanside, Long Island, says, 'mother' when he wishes to refer to the woman who gave birth to him. But a person from Warsaw, Poland, says, 'matko' when he wishes to refer to the woman who did the same thing for him. A person from Paris, France, says, 'chien' when he wishes to refer to a little, four-legged animal who appears to be Earthman's best friend. A person from London, England, says, 'dog' when he wishes to refer to the same animal.

7

"Each one of these noises forms a part of what is called the *vocabulary* of a language. The vocabulary of every language contains thousands of noises, since there are thousands of things to which Earth people need to refer. The English language, for example, has a vocabulary of about 650,000 separate noises which are called 'words' in English. Every time a new thing is discovered or invented, Earth people make up a noise that stands for that thing. For example, in recent years some Earth people invented a very primitive machine which makes it possible to see other people who are many miles away. In one part of Earth, America, the people think that this is so wonderful that they spend almost all of their free time staring at this machine. The thing is called (in English) a 'television set.' In the Yipounou language of Africa there is no way of talking about this machine because the Yipounous do not know about it. If they did, they would make up some noise which would then be the 'name' of this thing. The chances are that such a noise would not sound anything like 'television set,' because there are few noises that Yipounous make that sound like the noises Americans make. In fact, if an American heard a Yipounou speak, he would probably suspect that the noises do not mean anything at all. The Yipounou would probably think the same thing about the American's noises. Apparently, understanding each other's noises is one of the biggest problems of Earth people."

8

If our outer space reporter has enough training, he can probably write thousands of pages about language on Earth. Perhaps he will tell us more after he has returned and spent some additional time observing our planet. His statement above does, however, serve two purposes. The first is to suggest to you that it is both interesting and important to study things that we do not ordinarily think about. Speaking is somewhat like walking in that there is not one of us who can remember a time when we were unable to do either. Thus, we take them for granted, which means that we *do* them without thinking about *how* we do them. In one respect, this is fortunate; for if we had to think constantly about the way we talk, we would not enjoy talking as much as we do. People who stutter, for example, are painfully aware of their speech to a degree that we might find hard to understand. But in another sense, it is unfortunate that we take our speech for granted, for the less we know about *how* we do something, the more difficult it is for us to improve in doing it. If you are perfectly satisfied with the way you use language, if you are quite certain that you need no improvement, then you need not take any interest in knowing about how your language works. But if you are like the rest of us, it will be necessary for you to know a few things about language in order to improve the ways in which you use it.

The second purpose the Venutian's article serves is to point out that when we study something it is important to approach the subject with an open mind. To put it

9

another way, it is important to rely more on what you discover yourself than on what other people tell you. This is a valuable thought to keep in mind no matter what you are studying, but especially when you are studying language. Most of the things you will discover about your language during the next few months will probably be new to you, and some of these things may even contradict what others have told you. But if you will trust your own powers of observation, you may learn a great deal and have an interesting time doing it.

1) Which observations of the Venutian sur-
   prised you the most?
2) Did any seem unusually good?
3) Did any seem to be wrong? Completely
   wrong?
4) Is the Venutian handicapped because he
   hasn't studied Earth languages in Venutian
   universities?

1) Suppose you had discovered the cave pic-
   tured above. Write an article for the
   school paper on the topic, "A Day in the
   Life of a Caveman." Be sure to follow him
   through an entire day.
2) What parts of your article were based on
   specific things in the picture? What part of
   your article were merely guesses?

CHAPTER 2

Language and symbols

Rules, they sometimes say, are made to be broken. Similarly, suggestions are sometimes made to be ignored; so, after having just urged you not to rely too much on what others tell you about language, we hope that you will allow us to give you some information that will help you to begin your own observations and discoveries.

Language, as our Venutian observed, is noises. But all noises are not language. The sound of rain falling, the sound of glass breaking, and the sound of a bat hitting a ball are all noises, but they have nothing to do with language. Language is a special kind of noise—noise that *symbolizes* things. A symbol is something that stands for something else. A tin star worn on a cowboy's shirt, for example, stands for the fact that its wearer is a sheriff or marshal.

Almost anything can be a symbol if people agree to make it one. To Paul Revere one lighted lantern meant that the British were coming by land; two lighted lanterns meant that they were coming by sea. It could have been the other way around just as easily if Paul and his friend had wanted it to be. The meaning of a symbol is all a

matter of agreement. For example, if we all agree that each star in the United States flag shall stand for one state, then each star is a symbol of each state. It is as simple as that. If we should all agree that every five stars in our flag shall stand for one state, then we would need 250 stars to symbolize all the states in the Union.

Here is another example: If we all agree that automobiles must stop on green lights and go on red lights, then traffic policemen would give tickets to anyone who passed a green light. Perhaps that sounds strange, but if we all agreed to it, it wouldn't take very long before you were used to it.

Here is still another example: If we all agreed to make the sound "grumple" stand for that machine on which we see our favorite entertainers every week, then, in a short time, you would become accustomed to turning on the "grumple" instead of the "television."

In fact, if our Venutian visitor had been as observant as outer space people usually are, he would have noticed that the main difference between human beings and other occupants of this planet is that human beings are always making symbols, whereas other animals cannot. Symbols of our own making are all around us. Automobiles, clothes, rings, cosmetics, buildings—all these things and many others stand for various ideas such as wealth, position, marriage, youth, and religious feeling. Human beings live in a world of symbols which they have created themselves.

The first thing, then, to keep in mind about language is that it is noises that stand for things or ideas. It is *symbolic* noises. This part of language, as our Venutian wrote, is called vocabulary. But language is more than vocabulary. Suppose you heard the noises that follow: "own making around all us symbols of are our." These noises wouldn't mean very much to you, even though you were sure that you understood what each noise stands for. As they appear above, these noises are not language. But if you heard the noises made in the following way, "symbols of our own making are all around us," you would know very well what the message is, and you would know that the speaker was using language. What is the reason for this? The answer is that language is not only symbolic noises, it is symbolic noises *arranged in a particular way*.

Perhaps this can be made clear by an example from arithmetic. When you studied arithmetic, you undoubtedly observed that there are two kinds of symbols used.

One kind is called numerals. The other kind is called signs. Some examples of numerals are 8,4, 3. Some examples of signs are +, =, −. Now suppose you were given the numerals 8, 4, and 3 and asked to solve the problem. Your immediate reaction would be to say: "What problem? Do you mean 8+4+3? Do you mean 8×4−3? Or maybe you mean 4−3+8?" In other words, you wouldn't be able to get very much meaning out of the three numerals without help from the signs. But what exactly do the signs do? The answer is that the signs tell you how the numerals are related to each other. They tell you what you are supposed to do with the numerals. If a + sign is placed between the numerals 8 and 4, you know that you must add them. If a − sign is placed between them, you know that you must subtract 4 from 8.

Language also has two kinds of symbols: the noises that stand for things (vocabulary) and the noises that tell us how the vocabulary words are related to each other. The second group of noises (and this may surprise you!) is known as the *grammar* of a language. The grammar of any language, like its vocabulary, is a symbol system, or, if you prefer, a way of signalling. Grammatical signals are used to inform us of such matters as who did what to whom and when it was done.

For example, if you were to hear the words, "boy dog chase," you would know only that a boy and a dog are somehow involved in the act of chasing. You would not know who is the chaser and who is being chased. You would not know when the chasing took place or when it will take place or if it is taking place at the present moment. If these words are supplied with some grammatical signals, the entire matter is instantly clear. For example, such carefully arranged noises as, "the dog is chasing the boy," or "the boy chased the dog," provide you with a wealth of information that cannot be learned from merely hearing the words "boy dog chase."

In order to speak and understand a language, then, you must know two codes, its vocabulary code and its grammatical code. You must know these two codes, for example, in order to understand the following messages: "Fu ai tsi" and "Magister discipulum bonum laudabit." If you did know the codes, you would instantly know that the first message means, "The father loves the son" (in Chinese), and the second one means, "The teacher will praise the good student" (in Latin).

Of course, you do know the vocabulary and grammar of the language known as English. If you did not, you would be unable to speak or understand the speech of others. What you may not know is how these codes work, particularly the grammatical code, and this is what you are going to explore in the next few weeks.

EXERCISE 1

Rearrange the following word groups so that they make sense.

    1) home returned Venutian the saucer flying a in

    2) interested people readers his his article about Earth odd

3) Venutians people Earth interest
4) observations by amused Venutian the I was the of

1) What are the two codes of language?
2) Which one were you employing when you did Exercise 1?
3) Were you able to arrange any of the groups in more than one sense-making way?
4) If so, how can you explain this fact?

1) List specifically all the facts about the man in Drawing 1, and indicate how you determined each fact.
2) Try the same for the man in Drawing 2. How sure are you of the accuracy of your guesses? What prevents you from being completely sure?

CHAPTER 3

What is English?

In the last chapter, we told you a little bit about language. You will recall that we defined language in the following way: Language is composed of noises which symbolize things in the world and which are spoken in certain ways in order to show the relationship of one noise to another. Using this, for the moment, as our definition of language, what can we use as our definition of English? Well, we might say that English is a particular language. It has its own symbolic noises and its own grammatical code. Both of these are different from those used by people who speak other languages. Of course, if you have paid even slight attention to the English language, you have probably noticed that no two English-speaking people make their noises in exactly the same way. If you haven't noticed this, ask a classmate to say the words, "Elvis Presley" (or any other equally interesting words that come to mind). Then, *you* say them. If you listen carefully, you will hear a difference between his and your sounds. This suggests that in a certain sense each person speaks his own "private" language. But a more important point is that even though there are individual differences in speech among everyone of your classmates, there is enough likeness in their sounds so that each member of the class knows what the other means when the noises start.

This is an interesting point to keep in mind because English did not always sound the way it does now. In fact, if you could hear the sounds of the English language as they were made 1000 years ago, you would be quite sure that you were hearing a foreign language. The following line is from a poem written in England about 800 years ago: "Wel lange ic habbe child i beon a weords and ech a dede."

If you say these words aloud, it might strike you that they sound somewhat like the noises of the German language. This is no coincidence. The English language began about 1500 years ago. The island of Britain, which was then a province of the Roman Empire, was invaded by three tribes—the Angles, the Saxons, and the Jutes. They came from what is now Northern Germany. Until they came to Britain, the language that was spoken on that tiny island was called Celtic, a language somewhat like modern Welsh. But once they arrived, the Germanic tribes slowly drove out the Celts, some of whom fled to Ireland, Wales, and Scotland. The Celts who remained in Britain were forced, among other things, to learn the language of their conquerors. This early stage of English is usually referred to as "Anglo-Saxon."*

In the 8th century the Anglo-Saxons began to have troubles of their own. Vikings, coming mostly from Denmark and Norway, invaded the island and were so successful in their attacks that for a time a Danish king actually ruled Britain. But by the end of the 9th century, King Alfred was able to defeat the Vikings, and those Danes who remained in Britain finally settled down to live peaceful lives. By about the year 1000, the English language was a blend of mostly German, a little Celtic, some Latin (Latin having been the language of Rome), and some Danish.

In the year 1066, England was once again invaded and, this time, conquered by William, Duke of Normandy. His army was chiefly composed of men who spoke French. Thus, the influence of another language was felt by the people of Britain. By the 15th century, English had begun to sound something like the noises we hear and make today. For example, the following lines were written by Geoffrey Chaucer, an English poet, who lived in the late 14th Century.

* Thus the name "England," or "Angle-land."

He nevere yet no vileyne ne sayde
In al his lif unto no manner wight.

A modern English translation of these lines would be:

He never said nothing villainous about nobody
In all his life to no person.

It may not be terribly important that you remember the various conflicts and influences that helped make the English language what it is today. The important thing to remember is that the English language, like any language that has been used for a long time, has continually changed. And, as long as it is used, it will continue to change.

22

One of the reasons that English has changed and is changing so rapidly is that so many people speak it. Naturally, if only a few people who all live in the same place speak a particular language it is not very likely that the language will change much. If such a group remains together and does not have an opportunity to hear different languages spoken, each member of the group will learn to speak the language, almost exactly as any other member. But if 250 million people, living in all parts of the Earth, speak a language, then one must expect that great changes will take place.

Surely you have noticed that people from England speak differently from the way you do. So do people from Australia, from Ireland, from Scotland, and from other

parts of the United States. Each one of these special ways of speaking English is called a *dialect*, and sometimes the speaker of one English dialect will have a difficult time understanding the dialect of another English speaker. There is one English dialect that almost everyone who has gone to school understands. This is written English.

In a sense, writing is not really language at all. You remember that we defined language as noises, and writing is not noises. Writing is scribbles. But writing is a special kind of scribbles. It is scribbles that stand for noises. As we said before, human beings are constantly making symbols, and writing is simply one more symbol system or code that human beings have devised. Of course, not all languages have a written code. In fact, if our Venutian observer had made a study of writing while he was on Earth, he would have discovered that there are more languages on Earth that do *not* have written codes than there are languages that do.

But, fortunately, English is one of the languages that has such a code. We say "fortunately" since the invention of writing has enabled us to *remember* our past with considerable accuracy. People who speak a language for which there is no written code must pass on what they have learned during their lifetime by "word of mouth." This is not a very reliable method of recording history. You can test this out by playing a game that we used to call "Telephone." One member of the class whispers something to a classmate. The classmate, in turn, whispers what he has heard to a third classmate. The third whispers

to a fourth, and so on. When the last member of the class has received the whispered message, he tells everyone what it was. In most cases, you will find that in the process of retelling, the message has been changed so much that the last message has little connection with the first. Imagine how diffcrent the message would be if it had to be retold for thousands of years.

Thus, the invention of writing helped people to remember their history. And this helped them to improve their lives. If Isaac Newton had been unable to know what Johann Kepler said, it would have been almost impossible for him to figure out his laws of motion. And if Albert Einstein had been unable to know what Newton said, he would have had to start almost "from scratch." Without Einstein's discoveries, our space age could never have begun when it did.

We said before that no matter how much spoken dialects may differ, English writing is pretty much the same all over the world. This is generally truc, but we do not mean to suggest that writing has not changed through the years or will not change as time goes on. If you will recall the lines of Chaucer we quoted before—"He nevere yet no vileynye ne sayd/In al his lif unto no manner

CHAPTER 4

What is science?

Time, as the crow flies, passes very slowly. But as the space ship flies, a hundred years is not much longer than it takes us to snap our fingers. And so, to our Venutian friend it probably would have made little difference if he had visited Earth in the year 1659 (Earth time) or delayed his trip a week and arrived here in 1959. Of course, had he come 300 years earlier, he would have found the Earth and Earth people to be quite different from what they are today. For one thing, he would have seen no television sets, no radios, no movies, no refrigerators, no telephones, no electric lights, and no instant coffee.

Also, if our visitor had paid close attention to the behavior of Earth people in 1659, he would have discovered

that many people believed that illness (particularly mental illness) was a result of sorcery, that comets and eclipses were signs of coming disasters, and that witches were not mere fictions, but real people who could mix foul-smelling and poisonous brews. If you find it hard to believe that only 300 years ago Earth people still entertained such fanciful notions, remember that it wasn't until the year 1736 (less than 250 years ago) that the English Parliament finally abolished those laws which had been designed to punish witches. You might also be interested in knowing that our first president, George Washington, was "bled" to death by his physicians because they were apparently unaware of the fact that blood circulates through the body.

To put it simply, although 300 years is but a moment of time in the wide expanse of the universe, the past 300 years on Earth have been years of great change—years in which Earth people have almost completely altered their ways of thinking and, by so doing, completely altered their ways of living.

What was the reason for this? What happened to cause such important changes? The largest part of the answer can be given in one word—*Science*. Of course, we do not mean to suggest that exactly 300 years ago all men suddenly began to think scientifically and so immediately changed their lives. Obviously, things do not happen that way. In fact, the history of science is the story of a fierce and sometimes halting struggle to overcome superstition, tradition, pride, and ignorance—a struggle in which many honorable men lost their reputations, their possessions, and their lives. And you must not assume that the struggle is over. Nevertheless, it is fair to say that science has won its war, if not all its battles, and that Earth people, once having discovered science, can never return to pre-scientific ways of thinking.

But what exactly is science? This is not an easy question to answer, for many men have offered different definitions of it. But it is safe to say that, above all, science is a special way of thinking about problems; a way which requires, among other things, that investigators observe matters carefully before coming to any conclusions. For you living now in the 20th century, this requirement may seem perfectly obvious. But, as we have said, in the history of mankind, it is quite a recent idea. For example, Aristotle, a Greek philosopher who lived 2400 years ago, once wrote a book on the subject of physics. In his book, he said that if a ten-pound weight and a one-pound weight dropped from the same height at the same time, the ten-pound weight would reach the ground ten times faster than the one-pound weight. This was believed to be true for almost 2000 years. Why was it believed? It was believed because it seemed "logical" and because Aristotle had said it was so. And for 2000 years no one bothered to "check" it. When Galileo finally did "check" it (early in the 1600's), he found it to be quite false. His method of "checking" it was very simple. According to one story, he went to the top of the Tower of Pisa and dropped both a ten-pound weight and a one-pound weight. He observed that both objects reached the ground at the same time. As simple as this method may appear, it represented a great advance in Man's search for truth.

Thus, we may say that one of the basic rules of the "scientific method" is that careful observation is to be preferred over tradition, prejudice, or certain kinds of logic as a basis for discovering the truth. Of course, the word "careful" should be stressed almost as much as the word "observation." For if you do not make *careful* observations of the shape of the Earth, it is easy to assume

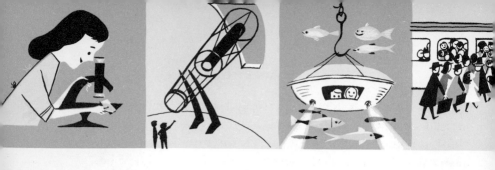

that the Earth is flat. (Does not "common sense" tell us that the Earth is flat?) But if you observe boats as they appear and disappear on the horizon, would you not begin to suspect that the Earth is not flat at all?

Another important rule of the scientific method is that no "truth" should be so cherished that it cannot be questioned or doubted if contradictory evidence is discovered. In other words, no good scientist ever says, "I am absolutely sure. The matter is closed."

There are, of course, other rules of scientific thinking, and it is our hope that by the time you graduate from school you will know most of them. The reason we have brought the matter up here is to suggest to you that the scientific method can be used in investigating almost any problem. This may surprise you, because when most people think of a scientist, they think of a man who investigates the behavior of fish (an ichthyologist) or the behavior of plant cells (a biologist) or the behavior of planets (an astronomer). But there are also scientists who investigate the behavior of people. These men are sometimes called "social scientists." Among this group, one will find the scientist who investigates the language of people. He is called a *linguist;* his science is *linguistic science.*

A linguist, like other scientists, must free himself from as many prejudices as possible so that he may investigate his subject with a clear head and sharp ears and eyes. For example, linguists do not assume that certain languages are "better" than others. Neither do they assume that a language is "faulty" because it does not possess certain features that some people think a language ought to possess. For example, some people believe that a word should have only one meaning. Yet we who speak English have no trouble, in most situations, in knowing whether a *run* in stockings or a *run* in baseball is being discussed. Linguists, then, try to describe what they find as accurately and as unemotionally as they can, just as astronomers try to describe the positions and movement of the planets.

Also, linguists try to make statements that can be verified or "checked" by other people. As scientists, they know that a statement that cannot be verified, even by indirect means, is either meaningless or useless. For example, suppose an astronomer were to say, "The planet Mars is more beautiful than the planet Venus!" By what means could anyone else verify the statement? Because there are none, we may say that this is not a scientifically useful statement. Of course, not all people are equally qualified to verify scientific statements. For example, if a linguist made a statement about the language of the Hopi Indians, we assume that most of you would be unable to say whether the statement was true or false. However, if a linguist made a statement about the English language, we assume that most of you would be able either to confirm or to deny it. For example, suppose a linguist said

the following: "In the English language, the word *boy* refers to one, but the word *boys* refers to more than one." Are you able to say that he is right or wrong? We think you are. Further than that, we think you are capable of doing more than just verifying statements. We think you can conduct an investigation of your own into the language you use—an investigation that would be exciting, informative, and in accord with the scientific spirit. Of course, you will need to concentrate. You will need to keep your head clear, and your eyes and ears sharp. And you must be willing to accept nothing less than the truth. This is much more difficult than it sounds, but if the linguists can do it, why can't you?

EXERCISE 1

When may a statement be called "scientific"? Below are several statements. As scientists, what kinds of information would you collect in order to decide whether each statement is scientific?

1. Junior high school boys are brighter than junior high school girls.
2. Junior high school girls are brighter than junior high school boys.

3. Students with high grades watch television more than students with low grades.
4. Men make better drivers than women.
5. Teachers who give easy assignments are students' "pets."

EXERCISE 2

If you were introduced to the following scientists, what do you suppose each might be interested in discussing?

1. an agronomist
2. a psychologist
3. an anthropologist
4. an archeologist
5. a philologist
6. a musicologist
7. a dermatologist
8. a botanist
9. a zoologist
10. a cosmetologist

EXERCISE 3

You may enjoy finding out what each of the following people do, and deciding whether or not you would call them scientists.

1. a phrenologist
2. an astrologer
3. a graphologist
4. a numerologist
5. a palmist

PART
II

*Exploration
of Form-Classes*

CHAPTER 5

The order of English

So much interest was aroused by the Venutian's articles appearing in *The Venutian Times,* that he was asked to write a book containing some of his other observations. In this book, entitled *The Puzzling People of Primitive Planets,* he wrote on a variety of subjects. Since he had discovered that Venutians are particularly curious about the many strange and amusing customs of the "teen-age planet," much of this book deals with these customs.

The following excerpt is from the chapter entitled, "The Peculiar Need for Order."

The Puzzling People
of PRIMITIVE PLANETS

"On my recent visit to the primitive planet Earth, I was struck by the need these people have for order. Indeed, they find themselves totally unable to behave in a satisfactory manner unless they have someone or something telling them in what order things should be done. Let me illustrate my point.

"If one looks at the number system used by any group or groups of Earth people, one immediately sees that its most important feature is its order—an order which Earth people feel they cannot break. Little children in school must count 1, 2, 3, 4, 5, 6. If a child counts 1, 3, 2, 5, 4, 6, the teacher appears upset and says the child is wrong. Apparently the only reason the child is wrong is that the teacher says so, and that 1, 3, 2, 5, 4, 6 is not in order. Why it needs to be in order is not clear. What *is* clear is that the teacher feels that the 'correct' order is important.

"Even the games played by these people show this need for order. In South America, North America, Japan, and a few other places a game is played in which a man hits at a ball thrown by another man. ·

39

Then, some other men chase the ball. After hitting the ball, the man runs around three white bags and back to where he started. For his team to get a point, however, he must go in order. Naturally, these white bags are always numbered 1, 2, and 3. They are never numbered 2, 1, 3 or 1, 3, 2 or 3, 1, 2 or in any other way which would be just as satisfactory. From what I have told you, it is very easy for you to guess in what order the bases must be run. On one occasion, I saw a small boy, just learning the game, run the bases 3, 2, 1. This brought laughter from his opponents and insults from his team mates. Personally, I often felt that there were advantages in running the white bags 3, 2, 1. It would certainly break the monotony.

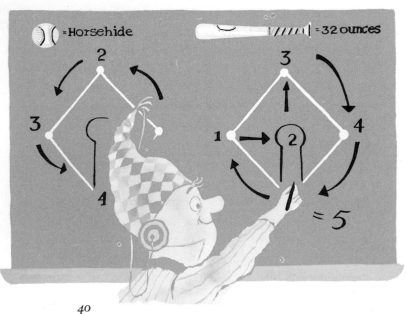

"Earth people also feel a need for order in their languages. Sometimes, however, they disagree on the order. For example, English-speaking people will say, 'that red house,' while Spanish-speaking people will say, 'that house red.' It should be noted that people who speak both languages will use the order of the language they are speaking at the time. In fact, it seems that when words from an Earth language are not in an acceptable order, the speaker cannot be understood by his listeners. Furthermore, English-speaking people may use the same words in two different acceptable orders and thereby express entirely different meanings. From this I conclude that the order of English words is of basic importance. Let me show you how this works with an example. The following are English words put in alphabetical order: girls, helped, mother, the, their. Now let me arrange the words in different orders. I will number them in the quaint way of Earth people.

1. girls helped mother the their
2. mother their girls helped the
3. the girls helped their mother
4. the mother helped girls their
5. the mother their helped girls
6. their mother helped the girls
7. their helped the mother girls

"There are many more possible arrangements that could be made of the words but I shall not list them as

41

most of them would not yield any meaning to Earth people. Of the seven sentences, above, only two have meaning for English-speaking people. The rest of the sentences mean absolutely nothing to them even though they are made up of common English words. Very strange, is it not?

"The two sentences that have meaning are rather strange, also. Simply by rearranging the words the speaker can completely change the meaning of what he is saying. In the first meaningful sentence (No. 3), the girls are helping and the mother is the one being helped. In the second one (No. 6), their relationships are reversed. It is, therefore, important in English that the order of the words be watched carefully or else you may say the opposite of what you wish to say."

Now here is something for you to do.

EXERCISE 1

Rearrange the following groups of words into English sentences. In most cases you will be able to make more than one sentence out of the group. Do not change anything except the order of the words.

1. people, guys, few, like, nasty.
2. football, Jack, the, is, player, best.
3. came, quickly, doctor, a.
4. trains, the, man, the, guard.
5. eaten, the, by, tiger, fast, was, man, the.

6. the, paint, ship.

7. come, you, tonight, will.

Now that you have read the Venutian's observation on the importance of order and have completed Exercise 1, what conclusions can you draw about word order in the English language? Write your conclusions carefully in your "linguistic science" notebook.

As you have begun to realize, and as the Venutian has pointed out, for words to work, as language, they must have an order or a "pattern." Perhaps you can discover something about the way words pattern in the English language.

The exercises that follow will help you to make some discoveries about word groupings in our language and how these groups of words pattern in our language. Do each exercise in your linguistics notebook.

EXERCISE 2

Place each of the words given below in the blank spaces found in Sentences 1 and 2. Make a list of those words that pattern in Sentences 1 and a list of those words that pattern in Sentence 2.

1. The ......?...... runs.		2. The boys ......?......	
man	girl	climb	player
swim	laugh	horse	car
race	dog	breathe	hide
elephant	crawl	grow	deer

43

Can you think of other words that will fit into the blanks above? How many can you think of in five or ten minutes? Make two lists, one for each sentence.

EXERCISE 3

Find at least ten words that can fit into the blanks in each sentence below (forty words in all). Words which fit in Sentences A and B should be added to your first list in Exercise 2. Words which fit in Sentences C and D should be added to your second list.

> a. Many ......?...... eat.
> b. Come into the ......?.......
> c. Children must ......?.......
> d. ......?...... the dog.

EXERCISE 4

Find at least ten words that fit into each blank below. In which of your two previous lists does each of these words belong? How did you determine this?

> a. The old gray ......?...... is clean.
> b. Some people ......?.......
> c. I ......?...... a few apples.
> d. Jack is planning to buy a shiny new ......?.......

EXERCISE 5

Read each sentence below carefully. Tell whether each blank should be filled with a word which would fit into List 1 or List 2.

a. ......?...... the car.
b. ......?...... a new hat.
c. Get the ......?.......
d. Airplanes ......?.......
e. Cook the ......?.......
f. Go over the ......?.......
g. This ......?...... is cold.
h. I am a ......?.......
i. ......?...... the ......?.......
j. ......?...... to the deck.
k. She ......?...... the cake.
l. ......?...... are hard to find.

You have just completed five exercises.

1) Can you make any generalizations, or statements, about the two lists of words you have developed to show how they differ? Write your generalizations or statements in your notebook. Discuss them with your classmates and see if you can come to any common agreement about the two lists.

2) Are your lists similar to those of your classmates?

3) How are they similar?

4) How do they differ? Perhaps you can give names to these two lists of words.

Keep your two lists of words in your notebook. You will need them in the next chapter and for future use.

CHAPTER 6

Form-classes: 1 and 2

In the last chapter you found two different groups of words. The main difference between them seems to be that the words in one list cannot take the place of the words in the other list. Another way of saying this is that *all words that pattern alike belong to the same word group*. In this chapter we shall explore more fully how a word patterns and how we can tell whether a word belongs in List 1 or List 2.

Suppose we take the sentence, "The boy runs." Words like *girl, man, dog,* and *woman* will pattern in the place of "boy," but will not pattern in the place of "runs." If you have not already named this group of words, it might be simple to call them *Class I* words. Words like *swims, sings, dances, grows,* and *reads* will pattern in the place of "runs," but will not pattern in the place of "boy." Naturally, they might be called *Class II* words.

Now let us see what happens if we do a little substituting of words. Look at the following sentences, all of which pattern, "The 1 2."

The boy runs.	The girl plays.
The girl sings.	The boy dances.
The man dances.	The woman reads.
The dog swims.	The dog runs.

We see nothing in these sentences that would upset our idea that words of the same group can be substituted for each other. Let us, however, consider the sentences below, which also pattern "The 1 2."

The dog dances.　　The cat sings.　　The rabbit fiddles.

These seem like English sentences, but they certainly express some unusual if not impossible ideas. If you think about it, you probably can come up with some perfectly ridiculous statements. For example, you can say, "The tree grows" and make sense, but try telling your friends that "The tree dances," or that "The tree runs," or that "The tree sings." Using the words in your two lists and using "The 1 2" pattern, try to organize some funny or improbable sentences.

In a sentence like "The tree runs," is *tree* a Class I word? Keep in mind that we have said that words that can be substituted for each other are of the same class.

We can say "The boy runs," "The girl runs," "The woman runs," but can we say "The tree runs"? Does "tree" really pattern the same way *boy, girl,* and *woman* do? "Well," you might say, "in fairy tales, dogs and trees sing. And they also dance, read, run, and do all sorts of strange things." Perhaps you can discuss this problem in class. Maybe its solution depends on what one means when one says a sentence "makes sense."

The exercises below might provide you with a clue to this difficult problem.

EXERCISE 1

Study the sentences below carefully.

The dog swam.	The chicken died.
The dogs swam.	The chickens died.
The lady left.	The boy danced.
The ladies left.	The boys danced.
The tree grew.	The red house burned.
The trees grew.	The red houses burned.

In these sentences, what happened to the Class I words? In each case, how did the change affect the sentence? Could the Class II word in each sentence be changed in the same way to get the same result?

Can you make a generalization about what can be done to Class I words? Try applying this generalization to all the Class I words you found in the last chapter. Does it work in all cases? Is this a good test for Class I words? Would a Class II word ever pass this test? If so, under what circumstances?

EXERCISE 2

Now let us look at some Class II words and see if we can find a way of identifying them other than the manner in which they pattern. Read the following sentences and see what changes take place.

49

The girls dance.	The woman cries.
The girls danced.	The woman cried.
The boys swim.	The cat plays.
The boys swam.	The cat played.
The boys fish.	The bus stops.
The boys fished.	The bus stopped.

Identify the Class II words in these sentences. What changes have taken place in the Class II words? How do these changes affect the sentences? Have any other words in the sentences changed? Could you make a similar kind of change in a Class I word to effect the same change in the sentence?

EXERCISE 3

We already know that one way of identifying a Class II word is to substitute it for another Class II word in a sentence pattern. Can you now make a generalization that will give you another way of identifying Class II words? Now write in your notebooks the generalization you have developed for identifying Class I and Class II words.

50

CHAPTER 7

Form-classes: 3 and 4

So far you have found two major groups of words. You have discovered that all words that pattern the same way can be classified in the same group or class. You have also found that one group of words has endings which signify "more than one-ness." You have discovered that words that change when the time of the sentence changes belong to another group or class. We hope you have given these two groups of words names. Perhaps you call them groups A and B, one and two, or, possibly at your teacher's request, nouns and verbs. What you call them is not important. It is important for you to know what the names stand for. You might be interested to know that some

Strutted   Tiptoed   Raced

linguists call these two groups, *form-classes*. Perhaps, before you finish your present study of grammar, you will discover why the linguist uses the term form-class. For now, however, we shall only tell you the names that linguists give to the two lists you have developed in the last two chapters.

Words that pattern in the blank in the sentence "The ......?...... is small" are called Class I words. Words that pattern in the blank in the sentence "The boys ......?......" are called Class II words. You may wish to adopt these names or symbols, or you may wish to keep your own. You should remember, however, that it will avoid confusion if your whole class can agree upon what names are to be used. For the rest of this book the authors will use the names that some linguists use because we have no way of knowing what names your class has chosen.

Waddled   Waded   Marched

Perhaps it has occurred to you that the two large groups of words (from now on we will call them classes) you have found are not the only large classes of words in our language. Let us look at some of the sentences we have worked with so far:

The ......?...... swam.   The boys ......?.......

Now look at the list of words below and try to fit them into the blanks of the sentences above. What do you notice?

tall	rapidly	sad	gay
pretty	young	sweet	gaily
happy	cautiously	green	quickly

Try the same words in the blanks in the sentence below.

The ......?...... boys ran ......?.......

53

3.=adjective
4 = adverbs

Can you think of other words that will fit in these blanks? Make a list of fifteen of them. How many new classes of words do you find? Name them. What do you notice about the words in one of these classes which might be a good clue for helping to identify this class?

If you worked carefully, you probably found two more form-classes. One class patterned *before* the word "boys" and another class patterned *after* the word "ran." Try the following exercises to test your understanding of how these new classes of words pattern.

EXERCISE 1

Find ten words that fit in the blank in Sentence 1 and ten words that fit in the blank in Sentence 2.

    1. The girls are very *Happy*...
    2. The doctor ......?...... ate his supper.

In which class does each of these words belong? How do you determine this?

EXERCISE 2

Read each sentence below carefully. Tell whether each blank can be filled with words from the first list you made in Exercise 1 or from the second list you made in Exercise 1.

    1. The ......?...... car is clean.
    2. Mary ran ......?...... to the store.
    3. The baker ......?...... baked the bread.
    4. ......?...... girls like ......?...... boys.

54

5. The ......?...... sun is sinking.
6. Few ......?...... cars run ......?.......
7. A ......?...... elephant ......?...... walked into the ......?...... cage.
8. Buy the ......?...... pocketbook.
9. The ......?...... tree reached ......?...... up to the sky.
10. The cat was very ......?.......

If you have read carefully the last three chapters, completed the exercises, and formed verifiable generalizations, you have learned a great deal about the four form-classes in the English language. Perhaps now would be a good time to re-examine your generalizations to see if they are still valid. The following exercises may help you.

EXERCISE 3

To which form-class does each underlined word belong? Tell which generalization you used to identify each one. There are thirty-three underlined words. Allow 3 points for each correct answer and see how well you can score.

1. The <u>old man died</u>.
2. <u>Slowly,</u> the <u>man walked</u> to his <u>house</u>.
3. In the <u>spring</u> the rain falls <u>steadily</u>.
4. <u>Good students try hard</u>.
5. <u>This</u> is the <u>time</u> to leave for the <u>East</u>.
6. <u>I am sleepy</u>.
7. The <u>red puppy trotted slowly</u> into the <u>yard</u>.
8. An <u>old man quickly ran</u> into the <u>new house</u>.

55

In each group of sentences below, the underlined words are from the same form-class. Tell which form-class they are from. You will not fail to notice—we are sure—that the same form class can have different positions in a sentence. Be careful to observe the position of one form-class group in relation to the position of other form-class groups.

1. A <u>leather</u> ball was stolen.
   The ball is <u>round</u>.
2. The tree <u>slowly</u> died.
   <u>Suddenly</u>, the tree died.
   The tree died <u>quickly</u>.
3. The <u>man</u> went home.
   The boy eats <u>hamburgers</u>.
   Wash the <u>car</u>.
4. Birds <u>fly.</u>
   <u>Stop</u> that car!

What generalizations can you make about the various positions form-class can take in relationship to each other?

Four rather short sentences follow. In each case you are asked to add words to expand the sentence. Place only a single word in each blank.

1.   *Birds sing.*
   ......?...... birds sing.

......?...... ......?...... birds sing ......?......

......?...... birds ......?...... sing.

......?...... the ......?...... birds sing ......?......

2.   *Wash the car.*

Wash the ......?...... car.

Wash the ......?...... car ......?......

......?...... wash the ......?...... ......?...... car.

......?...... wash the ......?...... ......?...... car ......?......

3.   *The men ate their food.*

The ......?...... men ate their food.

The ......?...... ......?...... men ......?...... ate their ......?...... food.

The ......?...... ......?...... men ate their food ......?......

......?......, the ......?...... men ......?...... ate their food.

4.   *The students are brilliant.*

The ......?...... students are ......?...... brilliant.

......?......, the students are brilliant ......?......

Return to the exercise above and label as many words as you can according to their form-class. Can you observe some basic English patterns? What are they? As a scientist you will want to look at all previous exercises as well as your earlier generalizations.

EXERCISE 6

In each sentence below you are asked to substitute words for one of the form-classes. Select words that meet the conditions asked for. Sentence number 1 is done for you in order to demonstrate what is wanted. For sentence one, we have listed a number of suggested words that could be placed in the Class II position to give a different or more exact picture of the boy's physical actions and/or his emotions.

1. *A boy walked across the street*

strutted	waddled	trotted
ambled	blundered	loped
stormed	hopped	dragged
tiptoed	staggered	streaked
hobbled	flew	dashed
skipped	raced	glided
charged	limped	waded
plunged	plodded	slipped

Write the complete sentence each time you make a substitution. In Sentence 2, substitute words in the Class IV position.

2. *The girls walked quickly.*

In Sentence 3, substitute words in the Class III position.

3. *A tall man approached the building.*

In Sentence 4, substitute words in the Class II position.

4. *The snake bit the man.*

EXERCISE 7

Write three sentences for each of the following patterns.

1. The 3 1 2 4 down the 3 1.
2. Few 1 2 4.
3. 4, a 3 1 2 the 1 in my 1.
4. A 3 1 4 2 a tree.
5. 3 3 1 2 into the 1.

EXERCISE 8

Write sentences in the patterns suggested below, expressing the emotion or condition asked for.

> Example: beauty and happiness
> The 3 1 2.
>
> The lovely girl laughed.
> 1. largeness and slowness
>   A 3 1 2 4 down the 1.
> 2. gaiety and lightness
>   4, the 3 1 2 and 2.
> 3. sadness
>   The 3 1 4 2 the room.
> 4. fear
>   1 4 2 for the 1.

EXERCISE 9

The following exercise is designed to help you see the possibilities for variety in the English language.
Below are eight words, two from each form-class. See how many sentences you can construct by putting the words in the following pattern: The *Class III Class I Class II Class IV*.

Class I	*Class II*	*Class III*	*Class IV*
cat	runs	large	slowly
dog	laughs	red	quietly

How many sentences could you make? Perhaps you feel this is too small a list of words on which to make a generalization about the variety of our language. If you wish to explore further, you might add the following four words to the eight you already have, and see how many sentences you can construct. Use the same pattern you used above. When you are through you should be able to make a generalization about the variety of our language. What gives our language this variety? Can you construct a formula with which you could figure out the number of sentences that could be made if still another word were added to each form-class?

Class I	Class II	Class III	Class IV
man	cries	lazy	loudly

Perhaps your mathematics teacher will be willing to help you with this problem.

CHAPTER 8

Word forms

Earlier, our Venutian friend gave some hint that he is an alert observer of the human scene. You have read some of the articles he has written for *The Venutian Times,* and you have read parts of a chapter in *The Puzzling People of Primitive Planets* that describes the strange and amusing customs of the earth people. Judging by the many words he writes on the subject, he is also an interested observer of the human scene.

Perhaps you will enjoy reading the following excerpt taken from *The Puzzling People of Primitive Planets.*

"All Earth people wear uniforms. In America, different groups wear different kinds of uniforms, and each uniform has a name. For example, the uniform worn along the ocean front in certain warm sections of America is called a 'bathing suit.' The uniform worn in the cities is called a 'business suit.' Young American girls wear something called a 'sweaterandskirt,' and young American boys wear a uniform called 'pantsandshirt.' When a young American girl marries a young American boy, she wears a 'gown'; he wears a 'tuxedo' (which, by the way, very much looks like a uniform worn by a North Pole bird called a 'penguin').

"It is required by law that these uniforms be worn. The law is called 'custom.' Policemen (also in uniform) enforce this law, but other people help, too. The law requires that the uniform for one place cannot be worn in another place. A 'sweaterandskirt' cannot be worn at the beach. A 'bathing suit' cannot be worn in school.

"The penalty for disobeying this custom law is very serious indeed. Sometimes those who refuse to wear the proper uniform are ridiculed; that is, other people point, stare, and laugh at them. Sometimes the 'criminal' is jailed. Often, he may even be considered crazy.

63

The Venutian is here describing something that you probably know a good deal about. Do you think he is accurate in all of his observations? What errors has he made? Has he missed some fine points?

You ought to discuss this matter with your classmates. Perhaps you would like to write an answer to the Venutian. You may be able to correct some false impressions, or maybe you can add some information which will be useful to the Venutian when he writes his next book.

Whether or not you have thought deeply on the subject, you certainly realize that the "laws" of custom are quite strong. The "laws" of language are equally strong, if not stronger. For example, you have already discovered that Class I words are generally not permitted to act as Class II words. Class II words are not permitted to act as Class III words, and so on. That is, they are not unless they change their clothing, unless they dress themselves up in a way that makes them look like the form-class they want to be. The exercises in this chapter will give you an opportunity to discover something about the special "uniforms" of each form-class.

EXERCISE 1

Directions: Fill in each blank in the sentences below by using one of the following words: easy, quick, rapid.

1. The car drove away ......?.......
2. That boy will win the race ......?.......
3. The basketball team won ......?.......

Do your sentences sound right to you? If not, why not? Fix them so that they do sound right!

What words did you change? What form-class does each word belong to in its *original* form? What form-class does each word belong to in its *changed* form? In what way did you change each word?

EXERCISE 2

Can all Class III words be changed (or "dressed") to form Class IV words? Can all Class IV words be changed to form Class III words? Use the lists you have in your notebook to determine the answers to these questions.

Choose twenty words from your list 3, and try changing each to a Class IV word. Write a statement about the method you use to make this change.

65

Choose twenty words from your list 4, and try changing each to a Class IV word. Write a statement about the method you use to make this change.

EXERCISE 3

We know now that some words must be changed if they are to pattern in a different way. It might be interesting to see whether or not these changes can give you some help in classifying words.

Below are three lists of words. Change each word in each list so that it will pattern as another form-class. Do not use any word in the form in which it is given. Change the words in each list according to directions.

List I

Change the words in this list to Class I words. Remember how a Class I word patterns.

> His *Class I* was good.
> The *Class I* went home.
> My *Class I* was evident.

To give you an idea of what you are supposed to do, we have filled in the first word.

	Class I
1. appreciate (II)	*appreciation*
2. apply (II)	
3. agree (II)	
4. attach (II)	
5. jump (II)	
6. achieve (II)	

66

7. run (II)	....
8. preach (II)	....
9. marry (II)	....
10. conquer (II)	....
11. pure (III)	....
12. superior (III)	....
13. weak (III)	....
14. happy (III)	....

List II

Change the words in this list to Class II words.

> That man will *Class II* you.
> That man will *Class II* himself to you.
> That man will *Class II* you to vote.

Class II

1. beauty (I)	*beautify*
	....
2. deputy (I)	....
3. terror (I)	....
4. pure (III)	....
5. vital (III)	....
6. glory (I)	....
7. false (III)	....
8. sharp (III)	....
9. soft (III)	....
10. strength (I)	....
11. hypnotist (I)	....
12. black (III)	....
13. power (I)	....
14. prison (I)	....
15. friend (I)	....
16. nomination (I)	....

List III

Change the words in this list to Class III words.
        He is very *Class III.*
        This is rather *Class III.*
        That is really *Class III.*

Class III

1. rely (II)   *reliable*
2. hope (II)
3. courage (I)
4. beauty (I)
5. wood (I)
6. dirt (I)
7. fear (II)
8. agree (II)
9. play (II)
10. detach (II)
11. faith (I)
12. value (I)
13. danger (I)
14. marvel (II)
15. glamor (I)
16. comfort (I)

When you have finished changing the words in each list, look them over carefully. Do you notice any similarities in word endings? List the endings that seem to be used with Class I words. Do the same for the other three classes.

These characteristic word endings can help you to classify words. We called these word endings "uniforms" earlier in this chapter. Some linguists call them "derivational contrasts," or *suffixes*. Of course, these suffixes alone cannot tell you what form-class a word belongs to; but they are, in most cases, important clues.

List in your notebook the suffixes that usually occur with each form-class. Also list the other method that you have developed for classifying words.

EXERCISE 4

There is another kind of word ending that helps to indicate a word's class. You have already discovered it and used it. It helps us to distinguish Class I words from Class II words. Do you recall what it is?

We can test Class II words by changing the time of the sentence. The ending which is often used to show that something happened in the past is "ed." An ending which indicates the present time is "ing."

This kind of word ending is called an "inflection." The inflections we have already discussed are only used with Class I and Class II words. There is a kind of inflection that we have not investigated before. It is a clue to Class I words. Time yourself to see how quickly you can discover it by reading the following sentences.

My *brother* is running down the street.
My *brother's dog* is running down the street.
Mother is in the kitchen.

Mother's hat is in the kitchen.
Jimmy wants to eat.
Jimmy's uncle wants to eat.

What happened to the Class I word in each case when it was followed by another Class I word? How could we use this as a test for Class I words? What do we generally call this kind of inflection?

EXERCISE 5

Still another kind of inflection is used with Class III words. Do the following exercise to see if you can determine for yourself what it is.
Fill in each blank in the sentences below with some form of the word indicated. Choose the form which patterns best in the sentence.

1. She is a very pretty girl, but her sister is even (pretty) .
2. Today is the (happy) day of my life.
3. That was the (hard) test I ever took.
4. This classroom is much (big) than the one next door.
5. The (fast) runner won the race.
6. My father is (strong) than your father.
7. I bought the (cheap) hat I could find.
8. Your handwriting is (good) than mine.

Can you answer the following questions?

What two inflections are commonly used with Class III words?

70

How do you determine when to use each of these inflections?

How can knowing these inflections help you to identify Class III words?

Suffixes and inflections are used so often by all of us, and we have become so accustomed to using them, that a sentence like, "The car drove away rapid" sounds "wrong" to us.

We can probably understand the meaning of this sentence, but the "laws" of language require that our words be dressed properly. Otherwise, the words that we use seem to form sentence patterns which are strange and awkward.

EXERCISE 6

Actually, the use of suffixes in our language adds a great deal of variety to our speech. Suffixes help us to "invent" new words. You might enjoy adding some new words to your own vocabulary by using suffixes to change familiar words to other forms. If you work as a group, your class may be able to "coin" a series of new English words. Perhaps a word invention of yours may become a permanent part of our language. In any case, it should be fun to try.

Change each of the following words into the class of word indicated in parentheses. For example, the word *eat* should be changed to a Class IV word, *eraser* to a Class III, and so on. Do this by using an appropriate suffix, or derivational contrast. Construct a sentence using each of the new words. Your sentence should give the reader a good idea of the meaning of your word.

1. eat (IV)

Although his mother told him to stop stuffing himself, he went *eatingly* on his way.

2. eraser (III)
3. window (II)
4. hair (II)
5. missile (III)
6. sky (II)
7. handle (III)
8. map (IV)
9. door (II)

EXERCISE 7

Next you will find an introduction to a story. (This one was *not* written by the Venutian.) Some of the words have been omitted. The number in the blank indicates what form-class the word belongs to. Make up your own words, using appropriate suffixes and inflections, and fill in the blanks. Then, finish the story in your own words.

Once upon a time, there was a ......1....... This ......1...... was very ......3....... In fact, it (he, she) was so ......3...... that it (he, she) always ......2...... ......4.......

One day while the ......1...... was ......2......, it (he, she) saw some ......1.......

PART III

Exploration of Function Words

CHAPTER 9

Determiners

A recent reading of the *Venutian Times* reveals that our space friend's visit to Earth has aroused the curiosity of many Venutian readers. One letter to the Editor of the Woman's Page reads as follows:

"Dear Editor,

"You have been very helpful to me with your suggestions on how to raise plants and children. I follow your column faithfully.

"A recent article in your paper called, "I Visited A Teen-Age Planet," has me worried, and I thought perhaps you could help me. The author of the article states that regular communication with residents of this juvenile planet (I believe it is called Earth) will probably be achieved in the very near future. We on Venus will no doubt send machines and tools to Earth as part of our Aid to Underdeveloped Planets Program. After that will come exchange visits of our citizens, which means that we will mix in their society and eventually even marry Earth people. Our galaxy has expanded so rapidly in the last two centuries that I am finding it impossible to keep my daughters properly trained. Originally, I taught them by following the advice of your column on Venutian Manners and Etiquette. Then, fifty years ago, communication with planets of the Pi-Solar System began, and I was forced to teach them the social customs of the citizens of those planets, too, so that my daughters could mix in interplanetary society.

"Now it seems I must begin again and teach them new rules of etiquette if they are to attain popularity in intrasolar social circles.

"In another twenty years, my daughters will be of marriageable age. I want them to be properly trained in order that they may take their place as leaders in whatever society they live. Would it be possible for you to pass on any information that you may have about Earth Etiquette, so that we mothers of Venus can continue the tradition of gracious, well-mannered, beautiful women, for which our planet is so famous?

"Sincerely yours,
Worried Mother"

In response to this letter to the Woman's Editor, our Venutian explorer has written a series of articles on Earth Etiquette. One article is especially interesting reading.

"In many societies on Earth there is great ceremony attached to the matter of making introductions. On being introduced to Royalty (a higher form of life than Man), many Earth people go through a series of physical exercises called "bowing." This is supposed to demonstrate the physical strength and agility of the person being introduced, perhaps to prove his worthiness to associate with Royalty.

"In the English-speaking cultures great importance is attached to the matter of who is presented first to whom. Oddly enough, the person for whom the society has the most regard is presented to the person for whom the society has the least regard. Thus, younger people are presented to older people, and men are presented to women. The accepted pattern of introduction goes thus:

> Introducer: "Miss Jones, I would like you to meet Elvis Presley."
> Elvis Presley: "How do you do, ma'am."
> Miss Jones: "Ohhhhhh!" (She faints.)

"Since they are constantly being introduced to men, the women of the English culture must become very adept at fainting. Venutian women who expect to be introduced in intrasolar society would do well to practice this art."

78

Your class may want to consider the following questions after reading the Venutian's account of Earth Etiquette:

1. How accurate are the Venutian's observations in regard to the etiquette of introductions?
2. Do you agree with his interpretation of why these procedures are followed?
3. Is the Venutian acting in a scientific manner when he attempts to explain the reasons for the behavior that he has observed?
4. What might account for the Venutian's conclusion that fainting is a part of all introductions between men and women?

You will find, as you proceed in your study of our language, that introductions are important here as well as in social activities. You have already found that there are four major form-classes. You have found that you can

79

tell which form-class a word belongs to by the way it patterns in a particular sentence. You have also discovered a
number of other clues which are helpful in determining
to which form-class a word belongs.

There are still other kinds of clues. One kind of clue
uses the idea of introductions. During the next few chapters you will have a chance to discover some of the clues
of introduction. You should be able to figure out for yourself what these clues, or signals, are because you use them
every day. It is possible that you have already discovered
some of them.

Below are five groups of words, each containing three
words which belong to the form-classes you have been
studying. Take each group of words and make it into a
sentence. Do not change the words you have been given.

(1)	man	looked	house
(2)	day	long	was
(3)	ran	street	dog
(4)	tree	quickly	grows
(5)	sky	flew	birds

What do you notice about the sentences that you and
your classmates have written? Were you able to use only
the words above? What are the differences between the
kinds of words you were given and the kinds of words
you added?

Classify the words you were given. Into what categories do they fall? Classify the words you added. Do
they fall into any of the categories you have studied?

You have discovered a new group of words that does not fit into any of the form-classes that you have already set up. Some linguists call this group "function words," but you may prefer to use another term. The name is not important as long as the whole class agrees upon the name to be used. Function words (or whatever you choose to call them) can be used as signals to help us identify the four form-classes we have already discussed.

Look back at the sentences you made from the five groups of words you were given above. Make a list of the words you added that came before a Class I word in your sentences. For example, given the words, "apples, grow, trees," you might have written: "Some trees grow apples." The word that was added was "some," and it came before the Class I word "trees." Thus, you would include "some" on your list.

See how many different function words you and your classmates patterned before Class I words in your sentences.

It may be that you could not list more than two or three different words from the five sentences you wrote. To enlarge your list, try the familiar method of substitution. See how many of the words listed below can be substituted for "the" in the following sentence.

The man looked into *the* house.

a	this	and	his
my	to	her	very
is	some	that	every

Those function words which pattern with Class I words are called "determiners" by some linguists. Determiners "introduce" Class I words. When you see a determiner it is a signal that a Class I word is coming.

EXERCISE 1

There are only about thirty-five determiners in common usage in our language. You have already discovered nine or ten of them. Can you discover all of the others for yourself? Try it by substituting words for "the" in the following sentences. Be careful that you are not listing Class III words. They sometimes pattern like determiners. Set up a test so that you can be sure you are getting determiners and not Class III words.

1. The apple is round.
2. The clothes are new.
3. The children can play this game.
4. The child likes to take medicine.
5. The dog lost the bone.

EXERCISE 2

Fill in the blanks in the sentences below by putting in a determiner from your list. Perhaps you can discover a few new determiners. Try not to use the same determiner too often.

1. ......?...... boys had ......?...... dog.
2. ....?.... people like rock and roll.
3. ....?.... students said they needed ....?.... time.

82

DETERMINERS

4. ......?...... girls have to clean ......?...... rooms
......?...... day. *(OUR, THEIR, every)*
5. ...?...... dentist has left ...?...... office. *(My, HIS)*
6. ...?...... men found ...?...... wallet in
......?...... street. *(THESE, ANOTHER, your)*
7. ...?...... women rode in ...?...... automobile. *(BOTH, ONE)*
8. ...?...... boy in the store had ...?...... dollar
to spend on ...?...... girl. *(THIS, NO, ANY)*
9. Not ...?...... teachers can drive ...?...... cars. *(any, other)*
10. ...?...... people go skating ...?...... day. *(Four, each)*
11. Put ...?...... car top down. *(HER)*
12. Fast drivers on ...?...... highways are
...?...... danger to ...?... safety of ...?......
people. *(many, another, the, many)*
13. ...?...... boys are excellent dancers. *(THESE)*

EXERCISE 3

Copy the sentences below and underline each Class I word.
Then tell what signals and clues you used to identify each
of the Class I words.

1. The cook eats now.
2. Cook some eats now.
3. Three runs came across home plate.
4. Run his car into the garage.
5. Take those horses over the jumps.
6. My horse jumps over the ditch.
7. That man runs a supermarket.
8. Ship the sails today.
9. The ship sails today.
10. The guards man the train.

83

11. The man guards the train.
12. The guard trains the man.
13. The train leaves promptly.
14. The leaves fall quickly.

A determiner is a signal to you that a Class I word is coming, but this does not mean that a determiner must always be followed *immediately* by a Class I word. Study the pattern in the following sentences.

This tree grows slowly.
This young tree grows slowly.

My book is missing.
My green book is missing.

Which words above are determiners? Which are Class I words? What kind of word comes between the determiner and the Class I word in two of the sentences?

EXERCISE 4

Here is a test sentence. From the list below select the words which can be placed in the blank in the following sentence:

Many ......?...... people drive cars.

young	swim	sleepy	quickly
easily	the	three	city
fat	ride	happy	my
lazy	boy	German	quick

What kinds of words can fit between the determiner and Class I word? What kinds of words cannot fit between the determiner and the Class I word? Don't be afraid to draw

84

on your own knowledge of language before coming to a conclusion. What statements can you make about the way in which a determiner signals a Class I word?

EXERCISE 5

Classify the words in the sentences below.

1. Some students like homework.
2. Many young people enjoy sports.
3. My tiny dog barks loudly.
4. Her busy mother burned the supper.
5. The new school looked clean.
6. That tall young man plays basketball.
7. Every young lady likes new sport clothes.
8. Those cruel men shot three rabbits.
9. Their kitten climbed several tall trees.
10. Happy students are the best workers.
11. Few tall girls like high heels.
12. His red car is new.

EXERCISE 6

Below is a list of words which can pattern as Class I words.

lady	company	student
Joe	animals	I
hat	Brooklyn	America
car	octopus	children
they	she	parents
it	Washington	Columbus
tree	sweater	he

Construct sentences using each of these words as a Class 1 word. Use each of the following sentence patterns at least once. The symbol *d* means determiner.

1. 1 2 3
2. d 1 2 1
3. d 1 2 d 1
4. d 3 1 2 3
5. 1 2 d 3 1

6. 1 2 4
7. d 3 1 2 4
8. 1 2 1 4
9. 1 2 d 1 4
10. d 1 4 2 d 3 1

When you have completed your sentences, consider the following questions:

1. Did you use a determiner to introduce every word from the list above?
2. If not, what words did you use without determiners?
3. What does this suggest to you about your classification of words? Should you change your grouping of Class I words slightly?
4. What does this suggest to you about your definition of determiners? Should you change it slightly?

CHAPTER 10

Auxiliaries

The articles and books written by the Venutian have become extremely popular among Venutians interested in people who exist on other planets. His *The Puzzling People of Primitive Planets* was re-issued in paperback and has sold many thousands of copies. His articles appearing in *The Venutian Times* have been widely read.

Because of the popularity of his recent series of columns on Earth etiquette, the Venutian has been hired to write a new series of articles. This feature is located in the comic section of *The Venutian Daily News,* and is called "Believe It or Not." IIere is a sample.

THE
VENUTIAN DAILY NEWS

THE NEWS
is
THE NEWS

"Believe It or Not . . . individual Earthmen are not identified by call letters,* as we Venutians are. This is impossible for them, for they do not communicate by thought waves. Instead, they have a very complicated system of identification, which is called 'naming.'

"In most Earth cultures an individual has a minimum of two 'names.' The first name is chosen by the parents, usually without much originality. In any one community there are a number of individuals with the same first name.

"The second name is known as the family name. In some cultures, children take the same second name as their father. In other cultures the second name is derived from the father's first name. Thus, Ole who is the son of John becomes Ole Johnson.

"These names are very important to Earth people.

---

* Scientists inform us that each Venutian "name" consists of four call letters. The first letter indicates the century of birth, the second letter gives the year of birth, the third letter tells the place of birth, and the fourth letter identifies the frequency on which the individual's thought waves are transmitted.

88

Some cultures believe that the name must be kept highly secret. They feel that the gods can harm a man only if they know his true name. So to protect themselves from this harm, they never use their true names. Instead they use another name to identify themselves in society.

"Some Earth people apparently think that a change in the name creates a change in the person. A man who wants to become famous in the acting profession frequently changes his name thinking that this will improve his acting ability. Teen-agers sometimes change their names, and adopt 'nick-names,' thinking that this will improve their popularity.

"This concern with the importance of a 'name' will seem strange to Venutians, but it is a fact. . . . . Believe It or Not."

Names as a means of identification seem so much a part of us that it may be difficult to imagine any other system. We give names not only to people, but also to all the other animals and even to inanimate objects which surround us.

Identification is important in our study of language, too. To date you have learned methods of identifying members of four form-classes. You have become familiar with determiners and can use them to help you identify other words. Let's look at another kind of function word, which can also be used as an aid in identification.

Study each of the following sentences and classify as many words as you can. Be prepared to tell what signals, or clues, you used in each case.

> That car should roll downhill easily.
> My hair may turn white.
> Track stars must run quickly.

Were you able to classify all of the words above? What did you call "should," "may," and "must"? Will they pattern in any of the following sentences?

> 1. The ......?...... runs.
> 2. The boys ......?.......
> 3. The ......?...... boys ran ......?.......

You may notice that "should," "may," and "must" almost seem to fit into sentence 2, but they do not seem to be quite enough. What kinds of words could you place in the blanks of the sentences below?

1. The boys should ......?......
2. The boys may ......?......
3. The boys must ......?......

"Should," "may," and "must" belong to another group of function words. What class do they signal? Some people call these words "auxiliaries." What might be some other good names for this group of words?

EXERCISE 1

Add to your list of auxiliaries by the substitution test. What words below can take the place of "should" in the following sentence?

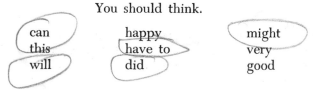

You should think.

can   happy   might
this   have to   very
will   did   good

Can the same words take the place of "may" and "must" in the sentences below?

> He may remember.
> They must wait.

EXERCISE 2

How many more auxiliaries can you discover on your own? Try finding words to fit the blanks in the sentences below. You may be able to find more than one word for each blank. Be careful that you are not using Class IV words. They sometimes pattern like auxiliaries. Can you set up a test to insure that you are getting auxiliaries and not Class IV words?

1. A person ......?...... sleep comfortably.
2. Several children ......?...... sing softly.
3. She ......?...... go shopping.
4. Only doctors ......?...... practice medicine.
5. I ......?...... like to roller skate.
6. I ......?...... go to school.
7. They ......?...... gone home early.
8. He ......?...... waited long enough.
9. I ......?...... return.
10. My friend ......?...... go to the movies every week.

EXERCISE 3

By now you should have a good list of auxiliaries. There are about twenty in common use. With the help of your classmates perhaps you can list all twenty.

Auxiliaries signal Class II words, but some words that are used as auxiliaries can also be included in another classification. Study the following sentences carefully.

1. My sister does the supper dishes.
2. My mother does like candy.
3. I do think clearly.
4. I do my homework easily.

Classify each word in the above sentences. Be ready to tell what signals you used in your classification.

What kind of word is "does" in the first sentence?
How can you be sure?
What kind of word is "does" in the second sentence?
How is "do" in the third sentence different from "do" in the fourth sentence?

Complete the following statement:
Auxiliaries signal Class II words, but some auxiliaries are sometimes used as ....?....................................

How can you tell when a word from your list of auxiliaries is being used as an auxiliary and when it is being used as some other kind of word instead? When you think you have discovered how to distinguish the way in which these words are used, write your idea (or hypothesis) in the form of a statement.

Now, test your statement as you work through the following exercises.

EXERCISE 4

Copy the following sentences, placing the word "yesterday" before each one. Notice what changes occur.

> I have learned my multiplication tables.
> We are going.
> That man has a new car.
> You can see the river rising.

1. What words changed?
2. What kinds of words changed?
3. Do these results require you to modify (change) any of your earlier conclusions about Class II words?
4. If so, how can you restate your earlier generalization to fit your present knowledge?

EXERCISE 5

You may have noticed that some auxiliaries are different forms of the same word. For example, *has* and *had* are forms of *have*. We say: "I *have* gone there," "He *has* gone there," "He *had* gone there." Can you supply the proper form of *is* in the following sentences?

1. I ......?...... swimming now.
2. You ......?...... swimming now.
3. He ......?...... swimming now.
4. We ......?...... swimming now.
5. They will ......?...... swimming tomorrow.
6. They ......?...... swimming yesterday.
7. He ......?...... swimming yesterday.
8. He has ......?...... swimming for a long time.

94

EXERCISE 6

A. What auxiliaries can be used in the following sentences?

    1. The birds ......?...... sing sweetly.
    2. Some people ......?...... dive from a high board.
    3. Many students ......?...... remember to do their homework.
    4. Those children ......?...... feed their pets every day.
    5. My friends ......?...... travel during their summer vacation.

B. What auxiliaries can be used in the sentences below?

    1. His dog ......?...... running away.
    2. The dinner bell ......?...... ringing.
    3. Our relatives ......?...... coming for a visit.
    4. Their football team ......?...... winning every game.
    5. Few people ......?...... hurrying to do their Christmas shopping early.

What auxiliaries can be used in this next group of sentences?

    1. Those men ......?...... wanted by the police.
    2. Several horses ......?...... left the stable.
    3. His father ......?...... gone on a business trip.
    4. Your sister ......?...... worked a long time for this money.
    5. That package ......?...... sent to you by mistake.

What similarities do you see in the Class II words in the first group of sentences?

95

How are the Class II words in the second group of sentences alike?

In what ways are the Class II words in the third group of sentences similar?

Can you make a statement about the kinds of auxiliaries that pattern with certain kinds of Class II words? Write down the statement that you would make. Then, be prepared to compare your statement with those that your classmates have made.

EXERCISE 7

You have discovered that some auxiliaries by themselves can act as Class II words. Use your list of auxiliaries and the sentences below to discover which auxiliaries can pattern by themselves as Class II words. Try substituting auxiliaries from your list for the blank in each sentence. The blank represents a Class II word in each case. Make a separate list of all the auxiliaries you find that can pattern as Class II words.

1. Mary ......?...... pretty.
2. The Saint Bernard ......?...... a large dog.
3. We ......?...... the champions in our league.
4. They ......?...... friends last week.
5. I ......?...... a good English student.
6. They ......?...... laundry at the laundromat.
7. He ......?...... oil painting as a hobby.
8. She ......?...... enough clothes now.
9. We ......?...... spaghetti for supper every Friday.
10. They ......?...... peaches and store them in the cellar.

When you studied determiners you learned that they signal Class I words. Moreover, a Class III word can pattern between a determiner and a Class I word. Now we know that auxiliaries signal Class II words. This exercise should help you discover whether or not a word can pattern between an auxiliary and a Class II word. Try to find words that will fit in the blank in each sentence below.

1. The rocket is ......?...... circling the earth.
2. I can ......?...... drive my father's car.
3. John will ......?...... win the tennis championship.
4. If you should ......?...... need me, I will come quickly.
5. Alice may ......?...... change her mind.
6. I will ......?...... wash the dishes.
7. They are ......?...... saving their money.

Study the sentences you have written, and answer the following questions.

What kind of word patterns before the blank in each case?

What kind of word patterns after the blank in each case?

Could you fill the blanks with words?

What kinds of words could you use in the blanks? How did you classify them?

Write a statement telling what you learned from this exercise.

CHAPTER 11

Intensifiers

Much earlier in this book, our Venutian friend observed that:

> ". . . if an American heard a Yipounou speak, he would probably suspect that the noises do not mean anything at all. The Yipounou would probably think the same thing about the American's noises."[1]

But our Venutian, as perceptive as he is, did not comment upon the real tragedy of our times: Even within our own country people do not understand each other's noises. Perhaps the most extreme example of this lack of understanding is in the differing speech patterns of the

---

[1] *The Venutian Times,* Sunday edition, Vol. 36, 458, No. 654, page 1.

"ancients" (adults, parents, teachers) and the "moderns" (teen-agers and children).

It is important for us to keep this difference in mind as we discuss the next type of function word. It is the hope of the authors that this particular chapter will provide a real service to mankind by helping the "ancients" and the "moderns" to understand at least one phase of each other's language.

The type of function word with which we are concerned is sometimes known as the *intensifier*. Perhaps a better name, considering our purposes, would be "illuminator," since these words will presently throw a bright light of understanding on the mysteriously different ways in which the "ancients" and "moderns" use the English language.

If this book were being written for ancients, a good example of the use of the intensifier (illuminator) would be found in the sentence: She is very extreme.

But since this is being written for a younger audience, much better examples must be found. At present, the two statements which come to mind are:

> He is real gone.
> They are way out.

There is a danger, of course, in using these as examples. Printing and binding a book takes a great deal of time. At the speed with which the English language is being changed by young Americans, it is quite possible that the particular words used above will soon become obsolete. Perhaps by the time you read this, the sentence in current use will be: She is jetly spacious.

But this possibility is something we cannot correctly predict; so we are forced to make use of the language of today, with apologies to the reader of tomorrow.

The type of word with which we are concerned in this chapter—the intensifier, or illuminator—is a word which can be substituted for "very." For example: This boy is very athletic.

Try substituting words from the lists below, and see what words can pattern in the place of "very" in the above sentence.

rather	went	can	most
pretty	too	real	little
some	game	true	really

Let us note here two more differences in the way ancients and moderns use the English language. An ancient probably would not use the sentence: This boy is real athletic.

He would say that "real" is not an intensifier, but a Class III word, as in the sentence: That is a real antique.

On the other hand, a young person might not use the sentence: This boy is most athletic.

He might say that "most" is not an intensifier (illuminator), but a Class I word, marked by a determiner, as in the sentence: That dress is the most.

The student of language might argue that both uses of both words are acceptable, as long as they are used frequently and are understood by the group using them.

Now that we have a brief list of some words that fit into this group, let's try to determine just what an intensifier does.

EXERCISE 1

For each of the following sentences list three words that might fill the blank following the intensifier.

1. He is very ......?.......
2. She is rather ......?.......
3. They are really ......?.......

4. I spoke very ......?.......
5. She ran somewhat ......?.......
6. I jumped too ......?.......
7. They swam quite ......?.......
8. We are pretty ......?.......

What kinds of words did you use in the blanks?

What kinds of words seem to follow intensifiers?

Write a statement explaining the job of an intensifier as a signaling device.

Now that we know what an intensifier does, we need to know how to test a word in order to determine whether or not it is an intensifier. There is a rather (very) simple test that is quite (very) accurate, and therefore pretty (very) useful. Can you guess what it is? If not, you are rather (very) blind.

EXERCISE 2

Underline the intensifier in each of the following sentences. Classify the word which follows the intensifier in each case.

1. Bill is a pretty common name.
2. Yesterday was somewhat cloudy.
3. I am an awfully slow reader.
4. Many people drive too fast on the parkway.
5. Jane was rather friendly this morning.
6. The cookies baked by the home economics class were quite good.
7. She is a real cute chick.
8. The team played rather poorly.
9. That music is real cool, man.

102

We know that intensifiers pattern with Class III and Class IV words. But we have not definitely determined that these are the only kinds of words with which we can use an intensifier. We need to test this further.

EXERCISE 3

In each of the following sentences, classify the word which follows the blank, and decide whether or not an intensifier can be used in the blank. Rewrite each sentence, giving one example of each kind of word that can pattern in the blank.

1. She was ......?...... singing.
2. He is a ......?...... dog.
3. They are ......?...... clever.
4. We like to run ......?...... fast.
5. That man can swim ......?...... easily.
6. Those students will do their ......?...... home-work tonight.
7. This food is ......?...... delicious.
8. The rocket was ......?...... circling the earth.
9. The English ......?...... is changing ......?...... rapidly.
10. Today's parents cannot understand their ......?...... children when they talk.

What kinds of words cannot follow an intensifier?

Can you use this knowledge to develop a rule that will help you to classify words more easily?

For example, what would be a good test to distinguish a Class I word from a Class III word?

PART
IV

Exploration in Review

CHAPTER 12

Word patterns

Certainly, the study of language is not simple, and it does not begin and end in the English classroom. You continually add to your knowledge of language from your reading in other subjects and from your contacts with other people.

Language, also, is a way in which people behave, and it may be studied the way we study any social custom. It has its special rules and its special type of organization.

Organization is so important in all kinds of human behavior that our Venutian friend has, naturally, taken a considerable interest in it. Because his observations often prove to be refreshingly honest, we have reproduced a portion of his article, "The Organization Planet."

The Organization Planet

"Earth people are extremely fond of getting themselves organized. They appear to believe that everything in life has to be in some kind of order, and they feel uncomfortable when things are not. There are social organizers, political organizers, economic organizers, and even organizers of other people's organizations.

"In America, both the Federal and state governments are highly organized. This kind of organization takes the form of arranging people according to their jobs. Each person has a specific job, and each person has someone above him who checks to see that the job is well done.

"American families are organized in much the same way. Older brothers and sisters tell the younger ones what to do. Parents check on all the children in the family. And there are groups of people outside the family who make sure that parents take care of their children properly.

"American fathers who work in factories or offices are also organized. They have a supervisor who directs their work. The supervisor is directed by the big boss.

"Even schools are organized this way. The work of the student is supervised by the teacher. The work of the teacher is supervised by the principal. This form of organization is found wherever groups of people get together regularly.

"Sometimes people are organized in other ways. At football or basketball games they may be organized according to the team they want to see win. The cheering sections for two teams may sit on opposite sides of the playing area. In schools, people may be organized alphabetically. (This term means an orderly arrangement according to the first letter in each person's last name.)

"Americans have still another type of organization for their eating habits. Food is eaten in a particular order. For example, few Americans ever sit down to a meal of chicken, mashed potatoes, and vegetable salad for breakfast. These foods are eaten later in the day. Foods which belong in the breakfast meal are

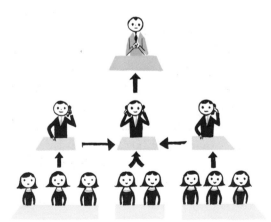

cereals and eggs. Furthermore, within a particular meal there is a special order of eating. Soup is eaten at the beginning of a meal. Dessert comes at the end. When children try to change this order by eating their dessert first, parents become very upset.

"Americans have not been content just to organize the *people* in an orderly fashion. They have even organized the highways and streets on which people and automobiles travel. Traffic lights indicate the time order in which people and automobiles may move. Automobiles must travel on the right side of the road. Where there are no special roads for them, people must walk on the left.

"These examples illustrate the extremes to which Americans have gone in their use of the idea of organization. Other primitive peoples show the same kind of tendency . . . ."

EXERCISE 1

The Venutian appears to criticize Earth people because they organize themselves and things.

1. Which of his criticisms, if any, seems most justifiable to you?
2. Are there any kinds of organization to which you object? On what basis?
3. Which of the Venutian's criticisms seems least justifiable to you? Why?

EXERCISE 2

As suggested earlier in the chapter, language is organized, too. The exercise which follows may help you to increase your understanding of that organization.

Put the words listed below into groups of two. You may be able to figure out mathematically how many groups you can get. Make as many groups as you can in ten minutes, by putting any two words together, at random. (For example: come man; go happy)

come	happy
boy	see
dog	funny
man	quickly
go	house

Now that you have made pairs of the words above, in what pairs does there seem to be some kind of organization? How many different kinds of organizations can you find? Which organizations would be useful for what purpose?

The grammar of a language is the way in which it is organized. Without this organization we are unable to get meaning from words. The vocabulary code is not enough. We must have structure, or organization. This structure, or organization, is provided by the grammatical code which we are now studying.

The fact that words are arranged in a particular order in our language should be a useful clue to us. In our attempt to find clues to help in the identification of form-classes, we have discussed function words (determiners, auxiliaries, and intensifiers) and word endings (suffixes and inflections). As we discovered in earlier chapters, word order is an important clue, also.

You have already observed a great deal about word order in our grammatical system. But you have not focused your attention upon this subject specifically. This may be a good time to draw together all that you have learned about word order through your investigations of form-classes and function words.

Scientists frequently collect data that they are unable to use immediately. They must learn to store this data temporarily, and use it in connection with a new problem after their initial investigation is completed. This is what you have been doing with many of the facts you have noted about word order. At this point, you should be ready to review these facts and to form some specific generalizations about word order.

EXERCISE 3

Think back through your work to date, and look back through your notebook. Ask yourself the following questions about each of the four form-classes:

1. What kinds of words pattern before each class of words?
2. What kinds of words pattern after each class of words?
3. Where in a sentence does each class of word fit—at the beginning or at the end?
4. What kinds of words seem to be found together rather frequently?

You will probably think of other important questions to ask. Asking the right questions can often be more important to a scientist than finding the right answers.

EXERCISE 4

When you have answered several questions like the ones above, you should be ready to form some generalizations to help you identify words by their order in a sentence. In order to check the generalizations that you have made, it is a good idea to use some additional facts. You might do this in either of the following ways:

A. Take a paper that you have written for one of your classes. Study each sentence and decide whether or not your generalizations still seem accurate. If they do not, you will have to modify them.

B. Study the following sentences. Attempt to fill in the blanks from your word lists. Decide whether or not the results agree with your generalizations.

1. Many ......?...... fly high.
2. ......?...... can be beautiful.
3. This ......?...... went home.
4. ......?...... can eat meat.
5. The ......?...... was dirty.
6. ......?...... move rapidly.
7. The dog ......?...... away.
8. Clowns ......?...... funny.
9. The grass ......?...... very quickly.
10. These pencils ......?...... sharp.
11. I ......?...... food.
12. Squirrels ......?...... easily.
13. Most people ......?...... regularly.
14. The ......?...... man was hungry.
15. Every ......?...... boy plays baseball.
16. My ......?...... mother went home.
17. Some ......?...... people drive cars.
18. All ......?...... students get good marks.
19. That ......?...... dog ran.
20. Four ......?...... chickens were caught.
21. Their ......?...... house burned down.
22. The hungry boys ate ......?......
23. Many people run rather ......?......
24. That boy swims ......?......
25. We must read these books very ......?......
26. ......?...... we will study poetry.
27. ......?...... the boy ran after his father.
28. ......?...... she left the room.
29. Students will ......?...... make mistakes.

30. You should ......?...... obey traffic laws.
31. The girls were ......?...... scolded by their parents.
32. I will go ......?...... ......?...... after school.
33. The dog ran ......?...... ......?.......
34. He ate his supper ......?...... ......?.......
35. They ......?...... completed their homework.
36. Foreign cars ......?...... run out of gas.
37. Mr. Johnson ......?...... dove into the water.

CHAPTER 13

Structural meaning

According to our friend, the Venutian, the time is not too far off when we may be able to communicate directly with other Venutians. Although *he* has learned English rather quickly, other Venutians will have problems because Venutians communicate entirely by thought waves. Happily, the Venutian has learned that there are great similarities between Venutish, the language of Venus, and English.

This similarity occurs in the structure of the two languages, not in their vocabulary codes. Because of this similarity, the Venutian has been able to develop a method for translating the basic signaling devices of Venutish into the similar signals of English. He has practiced this

method diligently until he is now able to transmit thought waves in English structure.

A major problem still to be overcome is vocabulary. The vast number of words in our vocabulary makes memorization of them and their meanings extremely difficult. The Venutian hastens to explain that this is not due to any inferiority of brain power on his part. The fact is that he has learned many English words. However, he cannot think these words without first thinking the similar word in Venutish. Therefore, his thought messages are extremely garbled and difficult to understand.

You will probably recall the limited number of function words and the limited number of varieties of inflections and contrasts. This fact makes thinking in English structure a much simpler task than thinking in English vocabulary.

The Venutian is very anxious for his people and Earth people to be able to communicate with one another. He

has made the following suggestions to help those of you who wish to be among the first to talk with Venutians:

1. A thorough knowledge of the structure of the English language, without reference to vocabulary, will be essential to any person who wishes to communicate directly with Venutians.
2. With a common understanding of the structure of English, Venutians and their Earth friends will find it possible to develop together a vocabulary which will be common to both.
3. This vocabulary will necessarily be limited to a reasonable number of words, so that Venutians can learn to think with these words easily.
4. The Venutian will be better able to determine what words will be most necessary for adequate communication if he has the cooperation of Earthmen in this process.

Therefore, our friend has requested that immediate steps be taken so that communication can be established as quickly as possible. These steps are two. One will be the mastery of the technique of speaking in English structure without using English vocabulary. The other will be consideration of the vocabulary which would be most useful for communication with the Venutians.

The method of preparation will be explained in the form of assignments from the Venutian. These assignments follow. Prepare well, and you may be one of the first communicators in inter-planetary language.

VENUTIAN ASSIGNMENT ONE

Make a list of the forty English words which you would consider to be the most important words for Venutians to understand in order to communicate. Be sure to have words from each form-class. Invent a word for each which would mean the same thing, but which would be easier to remember. Write a sentence for each word explaining why you think it is important enough to be included in the limited vocabulary which would be developed for inter-planetary communication. For example, you will probably want to talk about people. Therefore, you will need a word to symbolize what the word *people* symbolizes. Perhaps *Earthens* is a better word.

VENUTIAN ASSIGNMENT TWO

Practice your understanding of English structure with the following sentences. In each case although the vocabulary code is unfamiliar to you, the English structure is familiar. Classify each word, using each of the three tests—substitution, conversion, expansion—

1. The oogle boogled two weegles.
2. Many prinkles blonked dinkly.
3. Flooglement is wogling migly.
4. Bisage will be custed this kirness.
5. Our dulous dulage diggled doogily.
6. Rilk the tilks.
7. That gluity was glurring my gludable glurness gluppily.

8. Is the crummage credding very cranly?
9. Those faddles are rather fulmiful.
10. The plinkest plunk planked the plenkous plonkity plunkily.
11. His mirliful morrer may be mudching the megde.
12. Will the bugges mugge that very ruggable suggage?
13. Blaw the bloory blummage blantly.
14. Some meegles mig quite murily.
15. Riddlance is his rigglement.

VENUTIAN ASSIGNMENT THREE

Practice speaking and listening, using English structure with unfamiliar vocabulary. Work with one other member of your class. One person should say the first five sentences aloud, one at a time. Do not let the other person look at the book. The listener should then classify each word in each sentence. He may tell his classification or write it down. Then the listener should read the last five sentences, while the first reader listens and classifies.

1. Your wiggum has biggled.
2. Those oogable boogs doggled.
3. Do winkums sinkum quinkly?
4. Many rabbages rebbed very rubbily.
5. The twiggle is twimiful.
6. Is that smugger wigging his woggity?
7. Sangum the binkles.
8. That wog was a weegle.

9. Some very migiful tillums boodled.
10. The vatable crumness minkled riggly.

FINAL VENUTIAN SUGGESTION

You may want to try making up your own sentences to practice with your friends. This can be done orally or in written form. You may also want to include your forty invented words as the unfamiliar vocabulary. Continued practice will help to make you very adept at using English structure without reference to vocabulary. This will be useful to you when you are finally able to use the interplanetary vocabulary.

CHAPTER 14

Observation and classification

From a careful reading of his reports, you have probably realized that the Venutian is very different from Earth people. On the other hand, you may have observed some similarities between him and yourself or your classmates. For example, surely you have noticed that the Venutian loves to talk. Your teacher is almost certain to tell you that you and many of your classmates share this trait with the Venutian. You may have also noticed that the Venutian is quick to jump to conclusions. Do many of your classmates not "jump" almost as quickly? But

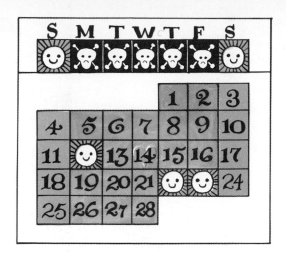

perhaps the most important similarity between the Venutian and you is that both of you know something about scientific methods of observation and generalization. The Venutian may not always be accurate from your point of view, but he does make an effort to observe and to generalize from his observations.

Another scientific technique which he has used is that of *classification*. For example, he has classified Earth as a "primitive planet"; he also has classified Long Island as a "remote place on Earth." You classify things every day, perhaps without thinking about it. You probably classify the days of the year into two categories: those days on which you have to go to school and those days on which you can have some fun. Perhaps you classify foods into two categories: those foods that taste good and those that taste awful. Some of you may use another kind of category, such as "fattening" and "non-fattening." Mothers tend to classify foods as either "good for you" or "not

good for you." Many arguments or discussions about your eating habits may stem from a basic difference in methods of classification. For example, the following "discussion" may sound familiar to you:

Mother: "I don't want you to eat French fried potatoes and soda for lunch."

Son: "But it's delicious."

Mother: "Never mind. You need something more nutritious. Why not have a lettuce and tomato sandwich and milk?"

Son: "But that isn't as good as what I like to eat."

Mother: "It's better."

Son: "But it isn't."

Mother: "Don't be stubborn. It is."

Son: "But . . . ."

Methods of classification in language study can cause discussions too, as you will note when you do the following exercises.

EXERCISE 1

Classify the underlined words in the sentences below.

1. <u>The happy people</u> cheered because their team had won.
2. <u>The Brooklyn Bridge</u> is very valuable.
3. <u>The school teacher</u> gave a difficult assignment.
4. <u>A pretty girl</u> walked by.
5. <u>Many sports cars</u> are being driven today.
6. <u>My red sweater</u> shrank when I washed it.
7. <u>Her science book</u> is lost.

Think about the following questions. See if you can answer them yourself. Be prepared to discuss them with your class.

How did you classify the first word in each of the phrases above?

How did you classify the last word in each of the phrases above?

What class of word should pattern between these two kinds of words?

What are some ways of testing, other than by word-position, to see whether or not a word falls into the class mentioned in your answer to question 3?

Can all of the words used in the middle of the phrases above pass the other tests?

EXERCISE 2

Rewrite each sentence below *twice,* substituting a Class IV word for the underlined word.

1. Yesterday I went there quickly.
2. Then, John ran home anxiously.
3. Mary always eats at home now.
4. Bill came there.
5. The dogs will race later.

In each sentence you have written, try to pattern an intensifier before the substituted word. Try to pattern an intensifier before the original underlined words.

Do you find it necessary to change your method of identifying Class IV words? Discuss this problem with your classmates and be ready to make some suggestions of your own.

In classifying words, you have used several methods. For example, you have observed the way a word patterns in a sentence; you have observed the form of individual words; and you have looked for certain function words which seem to be connected in a particular way with each of the form-classes.

The last two exercises raised some problems in classification. Perhaps you discovered that different methods of classification can sometimes give different conclusions. For example, consider the word "school" in the sentence, "The school teacher gave a difficult assignment." The way in which the word patterns would indicate that it is a Class III word. But it does not take an intensifier (or illuminator). No one says, "The very school teacher gave a difficult assignment." Also, you cannot say "school, schooler, schoolest." Apparently "school" has the form of a Class I word.

Consider the word "home" in "The boy went home." The way in which the word patterns would indicate that it is a Class IV word. But does it take an intensifier? Does it have an -*ly* ending? Does it have the form of a Class I word or a Class IV word?

If all of this seems confusing, you might find comfort in knowing that linguists are sometimes confused by this, too. In order to clear up their confusion, linguists establish a "hierarchy" of clues. This means that they arrange the clues in the order of their importance. Of course, different linguists work out different hierarchies. This is customary in science. Other people, discussing the work of a particular linguist, must understand and apply *his* system of classification.

For the purposes of clarity, you and your classmates should agree on one method of classification. For example, perhaps you might consider the *position* of a word in a sentence as the primary clue. Then, of secondary importance would be the *form* of the word, followed by the *function* word test.

Let us see how you might apply this hierarchy in classifying the word "college" in the sentence "The college student was smart."

1. How does the word pattern? Will it pattern in *all* positions as a Class III word? (For example, can you say, "The student was college"?)
2. What does the form of the word tell you? Can you say, "college, colleger, collegest"?
3. What function word, if any, can pattern with college? Can you say "The very college student was smart"?

In testing words to determine their form-class, you have been using three basic methods. They are called *Substitution, Conversion,* and *Expansion.* You probably have not been using these terms, but you have been using the methods which these terms name. Let us see how each method works in dealing with the word *silly* in the sentence, "The silly girls giggled foolishly."

The way in which the word patterns would seem to indicate that it is a Class III word. To check this classification, we might use the *Substitution* test. What other words can be substituted for *silly* in this sentence? *Happy, young, pretty,* and *gay* would all fit. You can think of many others. These words usually pattern as Class III words. Therefore, we can say that *silly* is probably a Class III word.

Now, let's try the *Conversion* test. When we use the Conversion test, we try to discover if the word will pattern in another position typical of its form-class. In this case, we would use *silly* in a different sentence pattern, such as, "The girls are silly." As you can observe, *silly* still takes the position of a Class III word. This fact verifies our classification even further.

In the *Expansion* test, we would place an intensifier before *silly* to see if the sentence still makes sense. The sentence would then read, "The very silly girls giggled foolishly." The intensifier fits. All three tests verify our classification.

As an additional check, you might look at the form of the word itself. Class III words can be inflected in a certain way. Can you say, "silly, sillier, silliest"? This is another kind of *Expansion* test, since you are expanding the form of the word. Perhaps you also noticed that the ending of *silly* (-y) is a typical Class III suffix. We should now feel rather certain that our classification is accurate. *Silly* passed just about every test we could apply for Class III classification. But what will you do when a word passes some tests but not others?

EXERCISE 3

Using as many tests as you know, classify each of the underlined words as belonging to one or more of the four form-classes.

1. The <u>atom</u> bomb is a frightful thing.
2. Nothing is so old as <u>yesterday's</u> newspaper.

3. The <u>dying</u> man groaned.
4. The <u>defeated</u> team sadly left the field.
5. My sister has a Mexican <u>jumping</u> bean.
6. The <u>condemned</u> man ate a hearty meal.
7. He had a <u>pale</u> blue Pontiac.
8. Many <u>baseball</u> players can throw a great distance.
9. The <u>singing</u> waiter entertained us for hours.
10. There is a <u>growing</u> disturbance in the hall.

EXERCISE 4

The first three exercises in this chapter have quite likely led you to the conclusion that in the study of language there are certain problems that are not easily solved. Below we have stated three more problems which we would like you to try to solve.

Problem 1

You have previously classified words like *the, my, his,* and *this* as determiners. Each one of these words patterns in the blank in "......?...... money is good." Now, observe carefully the four sets of sentences below:

    a. The money is good.
       The is good.
    b. My money is good.
       My is good.
    c. His money is good.
       His is good.
    d. This money is good.
       This is good.

Note the second sentences in *a* and *b* do not make sense, but the second sentences in *c* and *d* do make sense.

If *the, my, his,* and *this* are all determiners, why do *his* and *this* pattern as Class I words? Can you explain this fact?

Write in your notebook an explanation of this "problem." Be prepared to discuss your "answer" with your classmates.

Problem 2

Not all problems in the study of language are problems of classification. Almost every field of study presents investigators with problems of terminology. For example, you have used such terms as Class I, Class II, Class III, and Class IV. Other linguists use such terms as *noun, verb, adjective,* and *adverb.* Your task is to find out what the following terms mean and to relate them to the terms which are familiar to you. In order to do this, you will need to use a good dictionary.

a. NOUN	e. PARTS OF SPEECH
b. VERB	f. ARTICLE
c. ADJECTIVE	g. GERUND
d. ADVERB	h. GENITIVE CASE

Problem 3

Every language is grammatically redundant. This means that grammatical signals or clues are usually repeated several times within a single structure. For example, in the sentence, "These books are mine," there are three grammatical signals of plurality ("more-than-oneness"). Can you recognize them? In the Spanish sentence, "Los hombres altos están aqúi," there are *four* grammatical signals of plurality. Can you guess what they are?

In each of the following sentences, there is a Class I word. In the first sentence, the Class I word is signalled in *four* different ways. In the second sentence, it is signalled in *three* different ways. In the third sentence, it is signalled in *two* different ways. In the fourth sentence, it is signalled in only *one* way.

a. The establishments are doing well.
b. The roses smell sweet.
c. The boy is scholarly.
d. Rain is falling.

Can you identify all of the signals in each sentence?

In the following sentence, you will probably find it difficult to identify the Class I word or words. Can you explain why?

SCHOOL PLANS CHANGE.

PART V

*Exploration
of Sentences*

CHAPTER 15

What is a sentence?

How do you know when someone has stopped talking to you? The most obvious answer is that the noises stop. This observation, simple as it is, might provide you with the beginning of a definition of a spoken sentence. Such a definition might be stated as follows: A spoken sentence is that noise or group of noises that is preceded by silence and is followed by silence. The following is a written representation of two people talking in which, according to our definition, eleven sentences are spoken:

"Where are you going?"
"To the movies."
"What's playing?"
"The Return of the Teen-age Wolf."

136

"Who's in it?"
"Rock Corey, Thursday Frenus, and Franky
    Stravalone."
"Saw it."
"So don't come."
"All right."
"So long."
"So long."

Now there are a number of things that can be observed
about these sentences. For one thing, as we have written
them, they are a very poor representation of speech. It is
not likely that two people having such a conversation
would actually pronounce their words the way we wrote
them. For instance, it is probable that the first sentence
would be pronounced something like this: "Wahyagoin?"
Also, the last two sentences would probably be pronounced this way: "Slong."

Here, then, is one important difference between writing and speech: Spoken words are not necessarily pronounced the way they are written. Most people say,
"hamneggs," but the words are written as "ham and
eggs." Also, most people say, "would uv," but the words
are spelled, "would have." In short, writing is not, by any
means, an exact representation of speech. Writing only
approximates the sounds of speech.

Another thing to be observed about the sentences above
is that people do not speak punctuation marks. No one
ever says, Quotation marks capital letter W where are you

going question mark. Symbols such as (?), (") and (.) are only used in writing. They are not used in speech. But what are these symbols for? The answer is that they are used for the most part to represent (or symbolize) our "tone of voice." The symbol known as a period, for example, is generally used in writing to indicate that the writer has completed his sentence. In speech, the talker

simply stops talking. Of course, he may not stop for very long. To avoid confusing us, he uses another signal which tells us that he has completed his sentence. This signal is known as *intonation*.

For example, if a speaker wishes to signal us that he is concluding his sentence, he speaks his last word at a lower pitch than the others. Try this yourself. Say the sentence, "It is." Then say the sentence, "It is green." Observe the difference between the way you said *is* in the first sentence and the way you said it in the second. Now say, "It is green?" and listen to the difference between the way you said *green* in "It is green," and the way you said it in "It is green?" In one sentence your intonation was lowered; in the other it rose. Why? The answer is that by lowering your intonation you signalled us that you were making a statement; you were *telling* us that it is green. By raising your intonation you signalled us that you were *asking* us if it is green. If you think about all the signals that you transmit simply by altering, even slightly, the pitch of your voice, perhaps you will appreciate what a difficult task it was for you to learn language. Just think of the difference in meaning between the utterances, "What are we having for dinner, Mother?" and "What are we having for dinner? Mother?"

139

Another thing, then, that we may conclude about sentences is that there are different kinds of sentences. In speech we sometimes signal these differences by intonation, but in writing we signal them by making certain kinds of marks on paper.

There are many other things that can be said about sentences. Of course, you must remember that the definition of a spoken sentence that we provided at the beginning of this chapter is an incomplete definition. More important, it is certainly not a definition of a written sentence.

You might be interested to know that language scientists do not completely agree on the definition of a spoken sentence. There is, however, far more agreement on the definition of a written sentence.

By doing the following exercises, you may be able to discover something about what a written sentence is. Since you have read and written thousands of sentences in your lifetime, do not hesitate to draw on your knowl-

edge of written English, and, particularly, on your knowledge of English grammar.

EXERCISE 1

Let us assume that a sentence is composed of form-classes arranged in particular ways. Of course, not all arrangements of form-classes will make a sentence. Below are twenty structures. Which ones are sentences and which ones are not?

1. boys girls friends
2. boys jump
3. happy people and sad animals
4. in the tunnel
5. students study
6. the barking dog
7. the dog is barking
8. sing loudly
9. school is fun
10. people eat food
11. singing eating jumping
12. actually poor
13. he sings eats jumps
14. throw the ball
15. is school fun
16. come into the tunnel
17. far to the north
18. the growing plants
19. the plants are growing
20. the gloomis kraned the glom

Can you make some tentative statements about the differences between sentences and non-sentences?

Below are eleven structures. All of them would be recognized by most people as sentences. Identify the form-classes of which each sentence is composed. Then, perhaps you will be able to verify or at least strengthen any generalizations you have made about those arrangements of form-classes which we would agree to call sentences.

1. the man ran
2. students eat their lunch
3. the boys sit
4. the ship sails
5. ship the sails
6. Maris hit the ball
7. the ball hit Maris
8. roses are red
9. violets are blue
10. sugar is sweet
11. are you

Write in your notebook any of the generalizations you were able to make about how sentences are formed. Remember, your generalizations will be incomplete at this point. As you continue your study of sentences, you will want to refer to what you have written. Perhaps you will need to change some of what you have written. Perhaps you will decide to expand what you have written. It may even happen that you will need to reject what you have written.

CHAPTER 16

The nucleus of a sentence

As you worked on the last chapter, you no doubt were able to discover that Class II words play an important role in English sentences. You may be sure that others, besides yourself, have noticed the importance of Class II words as well. Indeed, the Venutian, our busy friend from outer space, has a keen interest in languages and the study of words, as we noticed in his article that was reprinted in an earlier chapter. Now, in response to many requests from his readers, he has written another article, entitled "Human Relationships," in which he has written at some length on the matter of Class II words and the part they play in sentences. Perhaps a glance at some of his observations will help you to think more deeply about your own observations.

An excerpt from his article follows.

Human Relationships
by V⅄∔4 mg.

"One of the most popular occupations of Earth people is that of searching for relationships. This means that they look for the connection between one thing and another. They do this, first, by observing things as carefully as they can; and, second, by talking about what they observe. Because no Earth man is intelligent enough to understand everything, the job of finding relationships is performed by many people. A special name is given to those who are searching for special kinds of relationships. People called *historians* are always trying to show the connection between present-day events and events of the past. *Psychologists* are always trying to connect what people do as adults with what they did as babies. *Doctors* try to find the connection between a patient's breakfast at 8:00 A.M. and the patient's sick stomach at noon. And *teachers* insist on connecting a student's lack of attention on Monday, Tuesday, Wednesday, and Thursday to his failing a test on Friday.

"Language, of course, plays a big part in the game of finding relationships. Moreover, language is especially important after someone has found a relationship, because then everyone uses language to argue about whether or not such a relationship 'really' exists. An example of this is in the discussion of whether or not there are life-like creatures on Venus. And believe it or not, most people don't think there are! Yes, Earth people love to talk about relationships. They write to their Congressmen; they argue with each other; they sue each other; and, in general, they have wonderfully good times discussing whether or not a relation that someone thought was there is really there.

"In order to show some of the relations that they have discovered, Earth people have found it desirable to do certain things to their language. For example, English-speaking people believe so strongly that there is a connection between 'yesterday,' 'today,' and 'tomorrow' that they are incapable of saying a sentence without giving some idea of *time* in it. They will say, for instance, 'I went to the movies yesterday,' or 'I will go to the movies tomorrow,' or 'I am going to the movies now.' Because Earth time is so different from Venus time, I have drawn an Earth 'time-line' which might give you some idea of how Earth people think things happen in the universe.

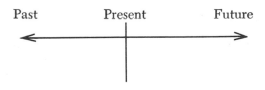

145

EXPLORATION OF SENTENCES

Before continuing to read the Venutian's report, you ought to give some attention to two matters the Venutian has dealt with. The first concerns his statement that Earth people "are incapable of saying a sentence without giving some idea of *time* in it." Just how accurate is that statement? Try to write a sentence which does not express some idea of time.

Second, you ought to try to fill in the "time-line" the Venutian has drawn. Copy it into your notebook. Then, using the sentence we have provided below, try to express as many different time relationships as you can think of. Unless we are confusing English with Venutish, we suspect that your Class II word will get quite a workout.

I	PLAY	WITH	HIM

Now, continue reading the Venutian's report.

"Time is not the only relationship that Class II words express. Class II words also show the relationship that exists among other words in a sentence. Look at the following sentences and see if you can discover, as I did, the relationships between the two Class I words in each sentence. Remember, the Class II word is the one that shows the relationship."

146

1. The fullback was my hero.
2. Boys are teenagers.
3. The boy kissed the girl.
4. The girl broke her doll.
5. The doctor cured his patient.
6. The lawyer was a woman.
7. He became a singer.
8. Policemen catch criminals.
9. Eisenhower was President.
10. Birds eat worms.
11. Gertrude is a dog.
12. Gertrude has a dog.

It appears that the Venutian has given his countrymen a problem to solve. We think you ought to try to solve the problem, too. The average Venutian needs less than three seconds in which to solve a problem of this kind. You may need somewhat longer. In order to help you, we will restate the problem. You are to examine the twelve sentences above very carefully. Each of the sentences is composed of a 1 2 1 pattern. In some the sentences the two Class I words are related in one particular way. In other sentences the two Class I words are related in a somewhat different way. Can you state what these relationships are?

Now that you have solved the problem, can you write five sentences in which the two Class I words, in a 1 2 1 pattern, refer to the same thing? Can you write five sentences in which they refer to different things?

You have found that there are at least two different kinds of Class II words. These will have to be named.

147

Some linguists call a Class II word a "linking" Class II word if it shows the following relationship:

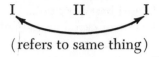

(refers to same thing)

If a Class II word shows this relationship,

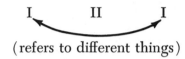

(refers to different things)

some linguists call it a "transitive" Class II word. Here, as in other places in this book, we would not want you to think the label is the important thing about the pattern you have discovered. Nevertheless, for the sake of convenience, you and your classmates ought to agree on what to call these different kinds of Class II words.

EXERCISE 4

Of course, all English sentences do not have Class I words on both sides of a given Class II word. Below are twelve more sentences. Examine each one carefully. Then indicate its pattern. You will find that not one of them patterns 1 2 1.

1. The boys are tall.
2. Girls are pretty.
3. The dog barked loudly.
4. Few men talk softly.
5. The cat seemed happy.

148

6. The girls were frightened.
7. Babies sleep quietly.
8. The children groped blindly.
9. The soldier stood quietly.
10. The soldier was quiet.
11. The detective looked carefully.
12. The detective looked good.

Answer the following questions.

1. What patterns did you find?
2. Which pattern may be most logically grouped with the 1 2 (Linking) 1 pattern?
3. According to our definition of "transitive" Class II words, how do they pattern?
4. What name might you give to Class II words which pattern 1 2 or 1 2 4 to distinguish them from "linking" Class II words?
5. What name might you give to Class II words which pattern 1 2 or 1 2 4 to distinguish them from "transitive" Class II words?

EXERCISE 5

Many people will often refer to *sit, set, lie, lay, rise,* and *raise* as the "six troublesome" Class II words. They are used correctly in the sentences below. How does each pattern?

1. He sits quietly.
2. He set his books on the table.
3. She will lie down.

149

4. She will lay her purse on the table.
5. The sun rises gloriously.
6. He raised his hand.

EXERCISE 6

Use each of the six "troublesome" words in three sentences. Check the correctness of your sentences by observing if their patterns follow the ones you discovered for each of the six words.

EXERCISE 7

1. Write five sentences which pattern 1 2 1. Have the two Class I words refer to the same person or thing. Use a different Class II word in each sentence. What name is given to this type of Class II word?
2. Write five sentences which pattern 1 2 3. Use a different Class II word in each sentence. What name is given to this type of Class II word?
3. Write five sentences which pattern 1 2 1. Have the two Class I words refer to different persons or things. Use a different Class II word in each sentence. What name is given to this type of Class II word?
4. Write five sentences which pattern 1 2 or 1 2 4. Use a different Class II word in each sentence. What name is given to this type of Class II word?

CHAPTER 17

Basic sentence patterns

At this point in your work, you have identified four different sentence patterns:

I.	I	2	I
2.	I	2L*	I
3.	I	2L	3
4.	I	3	4

Here is a difficult problem for you to solve, but we think you are ready for it. Three of the sentence patterns above are "minimum sentence patterns." This means that every part of the pattern is necessary in order to have a sentence. If any part of the pattern is removed, the structure is not complete. It would be like a square with only

* From this point on, the symbol 2L stands for a Class II linking word.

three sides or a triangle with only two. One of the patterns contains more than its basic requirement. In other words, one part of it can be removed entirely without destroying the basic sentence pattern. Your problem is to identify this sentence. But before you attempt to do this, do the following exercise.

EXERCISE 1

Below are five sentences. Identify those words in each sentence which are not an essential part of the sentence pattern. By "not an essential part" we mean that these words can be removed without destroying the basic sentence pattern.

1. The short pudgy man is my short pudgy brother.
2. The nasty boys rudely kicked my new car.
3. That stately blond girl is extremely beautiful.

4. Actually, he slept peacefully.
5. My unhappy father wants money very badly.

Now we want you to return to the first problem. Let us restate it for you. Below are the four sentence patterns you have identified. One of them contains more than the pattern actually requires. Which one?

1.	DOGS	LIKE	MEAT	I	2	I
2.	DOGS	ARE	ANIMALS	I	2L	I
3.	DOGS	ARE	HELPFUL	I	2L	3
4.	DOGS	SLEEP	QUIETLY	I	2	4

As you realize, basic sentence patterns can be expanded almost without end. Below is an example of a few ways in which a basic sentence pattern can be expanded.

		DOGS		LIKE	MEAT
	THE	DOGS		LIKE	MEAT
THE	HUNGRY	DOGS		LIKE	MEAT
THE	HUNGRY	DOGS	USUALLY	LIKE	MEAT
THE	HUNGRY	DOGS	USUALLY	LIKE	FRESH MEAT

EXERCISE 2

Take each one of the basic sentence patterns you have so far discovered and expand the pattern in as many different ways as you can.

Basic sentence patterns are composed of certain irremovable parts, and each part performs a special job. The parts are quite commonly given names. One name that is given to a particular part of a sentence is "subject of the sentence." Almost all sentences have a "subject." Your job here is twofold: (1) to discover how a "subject" may be recognized, and (2) to discover what a "subject" does.

Below are five different versions of a 1 2 1 pattern. In each case, we have underlined the part of the pattern that is called the "subject."

1. The <u>man</u> guards the train.
2. The <u>train</u> guards the man.
3. The <u>guard</u> mans the train.
4. The <u>man</u> trains the guard.
5. The <u>guard</u> trains the man.

What statements can you make at this point about the "subject" of a sentence? How can it be recognized? What is its job?

Write your answers in your notebook. Then proceed to the next exercise.

Below are five different versions of sentences following a 1 2L 1 pattern and five different versions of sentences following a 1 2L 3 pattern. In each case, we have underlined the part of the pattern that is called the "subject." Examine these sentences carefully.

1. The <u>man</u> is president.
2. My <u>son</u> is a doctor.
3. My <u>father</u> is an Elk.
4. The <u>lady</u> is my wife.

5. The <u>burglar</u> is my friend.

1. The <u>man</u> is successful.
2. My <u>son</u> is expensive.
3. My <u>father</u> is silly.
4. The <u>lady</u> is troublesome.

5. The <u>burglar</u> is careful.

Do you need to modify any of the statements you have made about "subjects"? Will you need several statements to describe what the job of a "subject" is?

Below are seven pairs of sentences. A careful examination of them might help you to add to your knowledge of how "subjects" may be recognized.

1. The boy runs.
   The boys run.

2. The floor seems dirty.
   The floors seem dirty.

3. This is my brother.
   These are my brothers.

4. The boy is cleaning the car.
   The boys are cleaning the car.

5. The ox is heavy.
   The oxen are heavy.

6. The desk needs a cleaning.
   The desks need a cleaning.

7. Ocean water washes against the dock.
   Ocean waters wash against the dock.

In each pair of sentences which classes of words change form? What causes the change? Can you write a statement describing how subjects are related to other parts of a sentence?

Identify the "subjects" of each of the following sentences.

1. There are five books on the shelf.

2. The man was elected president.
3. Here are my credentials.
4. The mouse was eaten by the cat.
5. Each of the boys is happy and proud.

Do you find you need to modify any of your previous statements about "subjects"?

EXERCISE 7

One of the important jobs of any scientist is that of communicating his results to other people. Your final task in this chapter is to write a report, as clearly as you can, on "Subjects of Sentences." Assume that your reader does not know what a "subject" is, but that he does speak the English language. After you have completed your essay, it might be a good idea to let someone you know read it—perhaps your parents or one of your friends in another class. If you prefer, you might pretend that you are the Venutian, addressing readers who are quite far away and probably entirely ignorant of "Subjects of Sentences." In any case, you should try to remember what the purposes of your communication are: (1) to let your reader know what kind of investigation you have made; (2) to let your reader know what your results are; and (3) to help your reader understand the results as well as you do.

CHAPTER 18

Types of sentences

"Earth people are creatures of habit!"

With those words, the Venutian began a fateful lecture on Station 402Q44, one of the more than three thousand stations broadcasting thought-o-vision programs on Venus. His lecture stirred up much interest, and letters poured in from all over the planet. These letters appeared to fall into three categories. First, there were those who felt that Earth people must be very dull if they behaved the way the lecturer said they did. Second, there were those who felt that Earth people had a happy, contented way of living, and that Venutians would do well to copy them. Third, there were those who felt that the lecturer made the whole thing up and that he should be vaporized.

Unfortunately, some of the most controversial parts of the lecture are lost to us forever. But we do have some parts of it which we are sure you will find interesting.

"Earth people are creatures of habit! On any particular day, at any particular time, you can usually find them at the same place you found them on any other particular day at the same time. There are some exceptions to this rule, but not many.

"If you should take a trip to Earth, you would know exactly what I am talking about. For example, suppose you were to spend five days in what American Earth people call a 'school.' First, I should tell you how to find a school. Schools are easily spotted because they are almost always made of brick and are surrounded by high, heavily wired fences. On the inside, you will find small square rooms which are filled with thirty or more seats. If you visited one of these schools, you would observe the behavior called 'habit.' To notice habitual behavior most easily, you might first pick out a student to study. Students are easily recognized because they carry books and talk all the time. Once you have selected a student, follow him for several

days. Observe him carefully from the time he enters
school each day until the time he leaves. Make notes
as to where he is, with whom he stays, what he is doing, and the time at which he does it. You will find, I
am sure, that he takes the same seat each day in each
of his classes. You will observe that he usually goes
from class to class by the same route. At lunch he sits
at the same table with the same people and they usually talk about the same things.

"There are other things you might notice, as I did.
You might observe that the student will treat each of
his teachers the same way each day. If he argues with
a teacher one day, he will usually argue with the same
teacher the next time he wants to argue. When your
student gets in line, he will get into the line at the
same place every time. You might observe that when
going down stairs he always takes the first step with
the same foot; when going through halls he may always
run; when going to class he may always be on time;
when eating he may always hold a fork in his right

hand; when writing he will always use the same hand; and when talking he may never wait for the other person to stop before he begins. There are many other habits which Earth students have. To list them all would be a job much larger than I wish to undertake now.

"Habits are very important to Earth people. Perhaps the only reason schools exist is to teach Earth children the habits of the adults with whom they live. As far as I can tell, the group known as teachers do nothing but figure out the best ways of getting young people to learn the habits of their society.

"I have been able to discover that Earth people also have certain habits in speaking and writing. For example, American Earth people habitually use three kinds of sentences. The way I discovered this, I think, is very clever and deserving of hearty praise. This is what I did: I recorded a group of sentences spoken by an English teacher in an American school. After the teacher spoke each sentence, I watched to see how the

161

students reacted. I felt sure that these students, being creatures of habit, would react the same way to the same kind of sentence. Below is a list of some of the sentences spoken by the teacher. After I list them I will tell you what these American students did upon hearing each one.

1. Good morning
2. Today we will study linguistics
3. How many form-classes are there
4. Open your book to chapter five
5. What does an auxiliary do
6. What is a symbol
7. Mary, quiet down
8. Jack, why are you late
9. Today's lesson is very important
10. Please listen carefully
11. There are probably three thousand languages on Earth
12. Bring your notebook to me
13. Close your books
14. Are there any questions
15. How do Class I words differ from Class II words
16. You have five minutes for this quiz
17. I am glad you all did so well

"The American students reacted to these sentences in different ways. In the case of sentences 2, 9, 11, 16, and 17 students . . ."

(During the transmission of this report to Earth the next section was lost. We continue with what seems to be the end of the section on kinds of sentences.)

". . . accounting for 16 of the 17 sentences spoken. The only sentence left to analyze is the first sentence. The reaction to this sentence was peculiar. The students said exactly the same thing back to the teacher. This I cannot explain except to suggest that it is just possibly another example of what Earth people call 'habit.'

"Having shown you the three basic kinds of sentences, let me make some other observations. These three kinds of sentences are not always said the same way. For example, one type has four basic patterns to it and each of these patterns has many variations. These different patterns and their variations make English a very interesting language and one in which a great many things can be said in a great many ways."

EXERCISE 1

No doubt the most important part of the Venutian's analysis was the part lost in transmission. Perhaps you can reconstruct what has been lost to us.

Write in your notebook what might have been included in the missing part of the Venutian's talk. Remember, he said he had discovered three different *kinds* of sentences, not patterns. Remember also that he discovered these by observing what the students did or said after the teacher spoke to them.

> Begin with:
> "The American students reacted to these sentences in different ways. In the case of sentences 2, 9, 11, 16, and 17, the students . . ." (did what?)

> What sentences would fit into each of the other two groups?
> What would the students have done after hearing these?

EXERCISE 2

Give five examples of each of the three kinds of sentences the Venutian discovered.

EXERCISE 3

Suppose the Venutian had grouped the sentences by listening to their *intonation* signals. Would the same sentences have been grouped together?

EXERCISE 4

Copy the sentences the Venutian heard. Punctuate each sentence.

164

CHAPTER 19

Variety in patterns

In the last chapter, you and the Venutian joined forces in discovering three different kinds of sentences. The Venutian classified the sentences according to the ways students responded to them. In addition, you classified according to their intonation. In this chapter, you will be asked to take a close look at "statement" sentences, "question" sentences, and "request" sentences.

EXERCISE 1

The sentences below are all statements. By now, you are probably quite familiar with at least four basic patterns of statement sentences. Write each of the sentences below in your notebook. Next to each sentence indicate *all* of the function words and form-classes of which the sentence is composed and underline the basic pattern of the sentence. Use the following symbol system:

Class I word	— 1	Class IV word	— 4
Class II word	— 2	Determiner	— d
Class II "linking" word	— 2L	Auxiliary	— a
Class III word	— 3	Intensifier	— i

Here are two examples:

d 3 1 a 2L i 3
The old *man can become* very *disagreeable*.

d 1 2 4
The *performer sang* badly.

1. Those men are fine lawyers.
2. Your idea is extremely good.
3. My brother hit the ball hard.
4. The child slept most peacefully.
5. Many Americans are men.
6. Some are women.

EXERCISE 2

Below are six more "statement" sentences. Can you identify the "subject" in each one?

1. Adam foolishly ate the forbidden apple.
2. The unpleasant youngsters smacked the horse.
3. The dutiful son washed his father's car.
4. The disobedient boy tasted his older brother's soda.
5. My mother fried two good eggs.
6. My father fired two bad eggs.

166

Each part of a basic sentence pattern has a special job to do and even a special name. You are, by now, familiar enough with the "subject" of a sentence and its various jobs. Your job here is two-fold: (1) to discover how an "object" is recognized, and (2) to discover what the job of an "object" is. Examine the following sentences carefully. In each sentence, the "object" is underlined.

1. Adam ate an <u>apple.</u>
2. The children smacked the <u>horse.</u>
3. The son washed the <u>car.</u>
4. The boy tasted the <u>soda.</u>
5. The mother fried an <u>egg.</u>
6. The father fired a bad <u>egg.</u>

Write in your notebook any statements you feel you can make about "objects." Try to answer the questions: How can an "object" be recognized? What is the job of an "object"?

EXERCISE 4

In the sentence, "Adam ate an apple," *apple* is called an object. *Apple* can be made into the subject if one writes, "An *apple* was eaten by Adam." Try rewriting the sentences in Exercise 3 so that the objects become the subjects.

What further statement can you write in your notebook that will identify objects?

EXERCISE 5

The four basic patterns of "statement" sentences with which you are familiar are:

1.	1	2	
2.	1	2	1
3.	1	2L	1
4.	1	2L	3

Pattern 1 cannot have an object for the simple reason that no word is needed after the Class II word to complete the structure. Pattern 2 is the pattern you have dealt with in the previous exercise. That leaves Patterns 3 and 4. In each of these patterns a word is needed after the Class II word in order to complete the structure. Such words are called *complements*.

Can you write a statement as to how *objects* differ from *complements?*

Can you write a statement describing the difference between the complement in Pattern 3 and the complement in Pattern 4?

Wash the car

Wash the
green car

Wash the green
car carefully

EXERCISE 6

Examine the four groups of sentences below. Label each word according to its form-class or function group. Use the symbols you used in Exercise 1.

Play the piano.
Play the old piano.
Play the old piano quietly.
Wash the car.
Wash the green car.
Wash the green car carefully.

Jump.
Jump quickly.
Jump quickly now.
Be good.
Be very good.
Be very good quickly.

Answer these questions:

1. What form-class words and/or function groups make up the basic pattern of the request sentences above?
2. Does an "object" play a part in forming any of these patterns?
3. Does a "complement" play a part in forming any of these patterns?
4. Are you able to find a "subject" in any of these patterns?

Test your answers to these questions by constructing ten "request" sentences of your own.

EXPLORATION OF SENTENCES

A third type of sentence is, of course, the "question." There is one very common sentence pattern for questions. Examine the following questions and identify their pattern.

1. Are the boys going
2. Have the cookies crumbled
3. Is her food ready
4. Was her brother happy
5. Are those girls laughing
6. Has the bell rung
7. Did the student call
8. Will the doctor come
9. Is it
10. Are you singing

Keeping the same basic pattern, rewrite the ten quesions above, putting a word before the first word in each sentence. Use at least five different words. Then answer the following questions:

1. What words were you able to add?
2. How did these words change the meaning of the questions?

Write your answers in your notebook. Perhaps you will want to name this group of words. We like to call them "question signallers."

Listening to conversation on a bus and using intonation as a guide, we were able to record the following questions.

170

1. What's your stop?
2. How do you know?
3. Is he friendly?
4. John is coming?
5. He is driving the bus?
6. Can you come tomorrow?
7. Does he work hard?
8. Where do you get off?
9. When will I see you?
10. Why are you shoving me?

Using the symbols you used in Exercise 1, show how the above sentences pattern. Use the symbol "q" for words that signal questions.

EXERCISE 9

In this exercise, you are given the choice of writing one or the other of the two essays suggested below. Read the suggestions and then choose one.

A. You have discovered three kinds of sentences: statement sentences, request sentences, and question sentences. It might be both informative and amusing for you to consider how often each type of sentence is used by some of the people you know. For example, if there are any three- or four-year-old children around your house, you probably have realized that their favorite kind of sentence is the question. As a young language scientist you should also be very partial to this type of sentence. Perhaps it seems to you that your parents favor the request

171

sentence. In any case, choose someone you know quite well. Then write an essay about him and his favorite kind of sentence (or her and her favorite kind of sentence). Of course, your essay should include some explanation of why the person favors one type of sentence over the others.

B. In doing the exercises in this chapter, you may have become aware of a great language mystery. We call it, "The Case of the Missing Subject," or "The Invisible Subject Caper." We are referring, of course, to the absence of a "subject" in request sentences. Write an essay about

172

this mystery, using whatever title you think suitable. Of course, you should include in your essay a description of what the mystery is, several examples, and the way a language "detective" might solve it, if, indeed, the mystery can be solved at all.

PART VI

*Exploration
of Expansions*

CHAPTER 20

Expanding basic sentence patterns

In the last five chapters, you have been primarily concerned with discovering something about basic sentence patterns. In this chapter and in the next three chapters, you will be concerned with the expansion of basic sentence patterns. Perhaps when you have worked through these chapters, you will be able to write a sentence like this one.

176

Although many people think otherwise, my
father's gray *dogs*, who have lived in our house
for three years, dearly *love* most of the charm-
ing *cats* who make their home in our backyard.

Now, this sentence is not a particularly marvelous one.
But it does give you some idea of how much can be ex-
pressed in one sentence by the expansion of a basic sentence pattern.

EXERCISE 1

Below are six basic sentence patterns, including four statement sentences and two request sentences. Your assignment
is to expand each one of the sentences, using any or all of
the form-classes and function groups you have studied thus
far. Here are two examples of what you are to do:

SUBJECT			CLASS II		OBJECT OR COMPLEMENT
	1		*(linking)*		*3*
	Sailors		are		seasick
d *3*	*1*	*4*	*(linking)* *i*		*3*
Many fine	sailors	sometimes	are very		seasick
				d	*1*
			Drive	the	car
		4		*d* *3*	*1*
		Carefully	drive	the big	car

Now try these.

SUBJECT	CLASS II	OBJECT OR COMPLEMENT
1		
Boy	sings	
1		*1*
Cats	like	worms
1	*(linking)*	*1*
Man	is	president
1	*(linking)*	*3*
Woman	is	beautiful
		1
	Study	books
	Go	

In Exercise 1, you may have noticed that the words you added were clustered about one or the other of the basic parts of a sentence. Thus, words like *big, green,* or *father's,* as well as determiners, almost always precede a Class I word. Such words are quite commonly called *modifiers* although the term *expanders* would be just as suitable.

Below is a single Class I word. See how many modifiers you can cluster around it. Remember, a modifier or expander serves to give added meaning or precision to the word it modifies. We have given an example of what you are to do:

178

Class I word

helmet

Example: The soldier's large, gray, steel *helmet*.

Now write sentences using these Class I words.

singer

teacher

shortstop

EXERCISE 3

Below are two Class II words. See how many modifiers or expanders you can cluster about each one. Keep in mind these two facts: (1) modifiers of Class II words are usually quite different kinds of words from those that modify Class I words; (2) modifiers of Class II words do not necessarily come *before* the Class II word. Here is an example:

Class II word

sing

Example: Now *sing* loudly.

Find modifiers for these Class II words.

skate

mind

throw

EXERCISE 4

Your answers to some of the questions in this exercise will depend to a large extent on your methods of classification. Thus, these questions quite possibly may lead some of you to give "correct" answers that are different from the "correct" answers of others.

1. Can you give any example of a single word modifier that comes *after* a Class I word?
2. Can you give any example of a Class III word that modifies another Class III word?
3. Can you give any example of a Class IV word that modifies a Class I word?
4. Can you give any example of a word with the form of a Class II word which modifies a Class I word?

CHAPTER 21

Prepositions

English literature is full of stories about families:

"Once upon a time there were three bears. There was the great big papa bear and the middle-sized mama bear and the little wee baby bear . . ."

And:

". . . so the prince and the princess were married, and lived happily ever after."

Then there was:

". . . Flopsy, Mopsy, and Cottontail were good little bunnies, and did just as their mother told them. But Peter . . ."

And you will also remember:

". . . when her stepmother and her two ugly stepsisters had left for the ball, Cinderella sat down in her corner and cried . . ."

We have heard these stories over and over again. Through listening to stories such as these and through living with our own families, we have come to understand many kinds of family relationships.

But our understanding of our families may be taken as much for granted as is our understanding of language. We are so accustomed to our families that we seldom stop to think about them consciously.

It might be rather interesting, then, to get a "Venutian's-eye view" of American families. Here, for example, is a chapter from the universally famous book, *The Puzzling People of Primitive Planets.*

"Most Earth people live in groups called 'families.' Some family groups are large; others are small. Americans generally live in a small family group. But there are other people, not living in the group, who also belong to the family.

"It is often difficult to discover the exact relationship between these other people and the small family group. Frequently Americans themselves do not understand the relationship, although they try to explain it. Here are some typical explanations:

'He is my sister's brother-in-law.'

'She is my father's cousin's daughter.'

'We are second cousins, once removed.'

'That woman is my husband's brother's mother-
    in-law.'

"Family relationships are so confusing to Americans that they even make up riddles about them. Here is one:

'Brothers and sisters have I none,
  But that man's father is my father's son.'

"Needless to say, many other societies are more advanced than Americans in their ability to explain family relationships easily.

"Usually, the method of explaining family relationships reflects the values of the group. For example, age is an important factor in Japanese society. This shows up in their language. There is no way to say 'sister' in Japanese. A child must say 'neisan' (elder sister) or 'imoto' (younger sister). Parents differentiate between their sons by age, also. A 'chonan' is the first son; a 'jinan' is the second son.

"Some Earth people value privacy. Those who do tend to build friendships very gradually over a long period of time. In such societies, people differentiate between family members or close friends, and mere acquaintances. These distinctions are apparent in their language. Spanish-speaking people say 'usted' for 'you' when speaking to people they know only slightly. They say 'tu' for 'you' when speaking to members of their family or close friends.

"In some societies, the sex of a person seems more important than in others. For example, boys are frequently valued more highly than girls. The language of these societies identifies a person by sex as well as by relationships. In German, a female cousin is 'cousine'; a male cousin is 'vetter.' Other groups may change the term used according to the sex of the speaker. A girl addressing her father will call him by one name; a boy will call him by another.

"In comparing American family groups with family groups from other Earth cultures, we must conclude that Americans are not much interested in their relatives, for if they discussed these relatives often, or had occasion to introduce them to their friends, they would realize immediately how clumsily their language does this task. Being efficient and inventive in their primitive fashion, they would probably develop a more adequate vocabulary. This has not been done. Therefore, it must follow that Americans do not discuss their relatives very often."

Do you agree with the Venutian's analysis?

Are his facts correct?

Are his conclusions logical?

Has he been jumping to conclusions, as he sometimes does?

Do you understand the family relationships that he used as examples? For instance, can you explain to the class who your "mother's husband's brother's mother-in-law" is?

Can you solve the riddle?

It is possible, of course, that Americans are not much concerned about defining family relationships. However, in other areas, we are usually very much interested in relationships. What news could be more important to a teen-age girl than Gloria's going steady with Marvin? What is more interesting to teen-age boys than the news that Harvey Moses and Tony Benino have been elected co-captains of the basketball team? Obviously, there are some relationships that are important to us.

Our language structure is another illustration of that fact. Perhaps the most important task of grammar is to explain the relationships among words. This is frequently accomplished by a group of function words which we have not yet discussed. They are called "prepositions."

Prepositions are words which pattern like "into" in the sentence:

The squirrel ran *into* the tree.

How many prepositions can you list in three minutes?

EXERCISE 1

Add to your list of prepositions by filling in the blanks in the following sentences.

1. We drove ......?...... the Brooklyn Bridge.
2. The Yankees played ......?...... the Dodgers.
3. Take the seat ......?...... the window.
4. I did my homework ......?...... lunch period.
5. Mary has a book ......?...... that locker.
6. The man ......?...... the car waved.
7. The pictures ......?...... the wall were painted ......?...... Jean.
8. I won't be ready ......?...... tomorrow.
9. She will walk ......?...... Carlos and Jack.
10. Someone took my book ......?...... my desk.

EXERCISE 2

Prepositions pattern in groups of words called "phrases." Classify the words according to form-class or function group in the following phrases.

1. into the water
2. beside me
3. over the rainbow
4. on a rainy day
5. between them
6. after the game
7. with Mary
8. in my old blue suit
9. on the birthday cake
10. at my friend's house

Can you discover a basic phrase pattern in the above examples? If so, write it down as a statement. Besides the preposition itself, what kind of word seems to be found in a "prepositional phrase"?

EXERCISE 3

Classify the words in the following sentences.

1. The children went in.
2. The children went in the boat.
3. The children went in immediately.
4. The children went in for their supper.
5. The children went in their father's car.

1. How did you classify "in" in each of the above sentences?
2. Which sentences above contain prepositional phrases?
3. Is "in" a preposition if it does not introduce a phrase?

EXERCISE 4

The short sentence "The dog ran away" can be expanded through the use of prepositional phrases. Here are some examples:

The dog down the street ran away.
The dog ran away from his master.

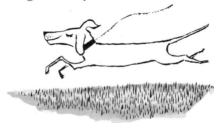

Each of the sentences which follow can be expanded by your adding prepositional phrases. Rewrite each sentence in as many ways as you can by adding phrases to different parts of the sentence.

1. The girl stood.
2. That table is clean.
3. Many people walked.
4. Jane took a bus.
5. Bill ran.
6. Close the door.
7. That car is a Chevrolet.
8. The cat ate quickly.
9. Her new coat is pink.
10. The flowers grew quickly.
11. Is there time?

EXERCISE 5

You have probably discovered that prepositional phrases can pattern in the same way as Class IV words. See if you can use a prepositional phrase instead of the underlined word in each sentence below, and still have the sentence communicate almost the same thing to the reader.

1. The _garden_ flowers smelled fragrant.
2. The _green-eyed_ monster roared ferociously.
3. The _patched_ trousers were out of place.
4. The _Madison Avenue_ bus was very crowded.
5. The _picture's_ colors were very bright.

What type of word patterns in the position of each of the underlined words in the sentences above?

Were you able to use a phrase to communicate somewhat the same meaning as the underlined word in each case?

What is the difference between phrases which form expansions like Class IV words and phrases which form expansions like Class III words?

EXERCISE 6

Using the symbols previously employed and "P" for preposition, write sentences for the following patterns. The phrases are underlined. Here is an example.

    d   1 <u>p   d   1</u>   2L <u>p d 3</u>
The man with the sunglasses looks like a famous
  1
star.

1. d 3 1 2 4 <u>p 1</u>.
2. 2 d 1 <u>p d 1</u>.
3. d 1 <u>p d 3</u> 1 2 4.
4. d 1 2 <u>p d 1</u>.
5. d 1 2 1 <u>p d 3</u> 1.
6. 1 2 <u>p d 3</u> 3 1.
7. d 3 1 a 2 1 4.

8. d 1 <u>p d 1</u> 2 3 1.
9. 2 d 1 4.
10. d 1 a 2 <u>p d 3</u> 1 i 4.
11. <u>p d 1</u> 1 4 2 <u>d 1</u>.
12. 1 <u>p d 1</u> 2 3.
13. 4 1 2 d 1 <u>p 1</u>.
14. 1 2 4 <u>p d</u> i 3 1.

       15. d 1 <u>p d 3</u> 1 2 4 <u>p d 1</u>.

CHAPTER 22

Conjunctions

The series of articles on Earth Etiquette written by our Venutian friend for publication on the woman's page of *The Venutian Times* is still popular. These articles have been seen less and less frequently, however, as the author now devotes a great deal of his time to counting the money he has made from his well-known book, *The Puzzling People of Primitive Planets*. Of course, when he does find time to write an article, his views are of as much interest to the scientists of Earth as they are to the citizens of Venus. As young scientists, you will probably be very much interested in the following article from the series on Earth Etiquette. This article is on the subject of marriage.

"Most Earth cultures have very strict marriage rituals. Some of these are short, simple rites. Others are complicated and lengthy.

"Americans have developed one of the longest and most highly organized rituals. American marriage rites are unusual for another reason, however. In the American system, a person frequently begins the ritual with one individual and completes it with another. In other words, the partner may change during the ritual. In fact, the partner may change several times during the ritual.

"There are three stages in the American marriage ritual. They are called the 'steadiment,' the 'engagement,' and the 'wedding.' The first stage is the one in which most of the changing of partners takes place. This stage begins in adolescence and lasts for several years. The second stage may last from a few weeks to a few years. The changing of partners in this stage is infrequent, although it does occur. The third stage involves a brief ceremony and concludes the American ritual of marriage.

"Americans are very fond of using symbols to denote the status of individuals in society. Naturally, they have symbols to indicate each stage of the marriage ritual.

A boy and girl who are 'going steady' may advertise their status through the use of many different symbols. They may wear identical sweaters. They may write 'Jane + John' on their books or their hats or their skin. The symbols used change with each generation. A girl who is 'engaged' generally advertises her status by wearing a certain kind of ring. The boy is not required to indicate his status during the engagement period. During the 'wedding' ceremony an exchange of 'wedding rings' usually takes place. These rings symbolize the married status which the couple has reached.

"The development of these symbols indicates the importance which Americans attach to knowing which people belong together. The social status of a person determines to some extent the way in which he is treated by others. The use of symbols such as rings points out a connection or link between two people and helps to inform others of their social status."

Earthmen who are interested in sociology might read this article to gain a new perspective on social customs. A linguistic scientist like yourself might want to consider whether the English language has any parallel to this social custom, since you have already discovered many other similarities between social custom and language. Can you discover a group of function words which indicates a connection or a "togetherness" between two words or groups of words? Study the following excerpts from popular English "literature," and see what ideas you get.

"Jack and Jill went up the hill . . ."
"Hey diddle diddle! the cat and the fiddle . . ."
". . . with silver bells and cockle shells
    and pretty maids all in a row."
". . . he stuck in his thumb,
    and pulled out a plum . . ."
". . . the pig was eat,
    and Tom was beat,
    and Tom went crying down the street."

If you classify the words in the nursery rhymes above, you will find some similarities in patterns. What word connects the similar patterns in each case? This word is the most commonly used one in our new function group. It and words like it are called "conjunctions."

EXERCISE 1

Study the following sentences, and classify the words. In each case where a conjunction appears, it is underlined. Be ready to tell what job the conjunction performs in sentences.

1. Mary went to the party.
2. Mary <u>and</u> Janet slid down the hill.
3. This book can be read quickly.
4. My pen <u>and</u> his pencil are missing.
5. Some young people drive safely.
6. Many cold days <u>and</u> some warm ones occur in the winter.
7. Is the sun shining today?
8. Are you <u>and</u> your friend going home?
9. When was the telephone invented?
10. Why did Lewis <u>and</u> Clark explore the West?

In the sentences above, what part of the sentence pattern is changed by the use of the conjunction? What effect does the addition of the conjunction have on the total sentence?

As you have probably concluded, conjunctions are used as another means of expanding the basic sentence pattern. When a conjunction is used with the subject of a sentence to form an expanded pattern, we call the result a "compound" subject. A conjunction used to expand the pattern with a Class II word forms a "compound" predicate. The basic pattern with which we have been working in previous chapters contains a "simple" subject and a "simple" predicate—that is, one of each.

EXERCISE 2

Study the sentences below. Indicate (1) what part is the subject, (2) what part is the predicate, (3) if the subject is simple or compound, and (4) if the predicate is simple or compound.

1. John came to school late this morning.
2. Bacteria and amoeba are microscopic forms of life.
3. Students at the class picnic went swimming and hiking.
4. The Hatfields and the McCoys shot and killed each other.
5. Did Marquette and Joliet explore the St. Lawrence and the Mississippi?

EXERCISE 3

Now that you have some understanding of how conjunctions contribute to our language, try to identify some more conjunctions. *And* is one of the most commonly used, but it is not the only one. See if you can identify some other conjunctions in the following sentences. Remember that conjunctions expand the sentence pattern by connecting similar words or groups of words.

List all the conjunctions you can find in the following sentences. Write them in your notebook.

1. The Dodgers or the Yankees will win the next World Series.
2. You should not chew gum or talk in class.
3. Either Albie Snedley or Jacky Wilson will star in the movie, "Pirate Chasers."

196

4. Did you pass or fail your exams?
5. Neither my father nor my mother can dance the twist.
6. Tired but happy, the winning team left the the field.
7. I went straight home, but James stayed at school.
8. Wash the dishes and make your bed.
9. Both Helen and Jane may wear lipstick.
10. Over the meadow and through the wood to Grandmother's house we go.
11. The sentry looked neither to the left nor to the right.
12. I must earn some money, or I can't take you to the dance.
13. Betty has a new dress, and I want one, too.
14. Our team won the game because Harry scored three touchdowns.

What parts of a sentence can be expanded by use of conjunctions besides Class I words in the subject and Class II words in the predicate?

Look at sentences 7, 8, 12, 13, and 14 in the exercise above. How do they differ from the other sentences? What parts of the sentence are connected by the conjunction in each case? Can you think of a good name for this kind of sentence?

EXERCISE 4

For each of the following basic sentence patterns, construct a sentence. Then expand it in three different ways through the use of a conjunction. An example follows:

Pattern: d 3 1 2 4

Sentence: The sly fox ate greedily.

Expansion 1: The sly fox and the wily wolf ate greedily.

Expansion 2: The sly fox ate greedily but watchfully.

Expansion 3: The sly fox ate greedily and the foolish crow watched sadly.

1. d 1 <u>p d 1</u> 2.   3. 1 2 <u>p d 1</u> 4.

2. d 3 1 a 2 4.   4. a d 1 2 d 1?

             5. 2 d 1 <u>p d 1</u>.

EXERCISE 5

Starting with the following four basic sentence patterns, expand the patterns in any way you like. The basic methods of expansion that we have learned so far include using Class III words, Class IV words, determiners, intensifiers, auxiliaries, prepositional phrases, and conjunctions. See how many different types of expansion you can use with each sentence pattern.

1	2	1
1	2L	1
1	2L	3
1	2	

CHAPTER 23

Subordinators

Physics teaches us that warm air expands and cold air contracts. More precisely, it teaches us that when air is heated, molecules move more rapidly and, thereby, take up more space. When air is cooled, molecules move more slowly and take up less space.

The Venutian, who knew all of this before he ever visited our planet, has developed a humorous theory about the expansion and contraction of language patterns. The theory can be stated in the following way: English sentence patterns expand in direct proportion to the rising temperature of the speaker. Conversely, sentence patterns contract in direct proportion to the falling temperature of the speaker.

Thus, as the Venutian has noticed, when a person "warms to his subject," he speaks more rapidly and his sentences become longer. When an argument gets "hot," words tumble out in great quantities from all participants.

On the other hand, when someone is giving you the "cold shoulder," he will speak to you only briefly and in very short sentences. A girl who is treating her boy friend to a "deep freeze" may not be speaking to him at all; or, if she does, her sentences may be limited to something like, "Is that so?"

We would not care to vouch for the accuracy of the Venutian's theory. Like most Earth people, he has his frivolous moments. But we are certain that the expansion and contraction of English sentence patterns are as important a matter to the linguist as the expansion and contraction of air are to the physicist. Therefore, in this chapter, you will be asked to investigate some methods of expansion which you have not yet studied.

EXERCISE 1

Find as many words as you can that will substitute for the underlined word in each sentence below.

1. Sam went to the store <u>because</u> he needed a new baseball bat.
2. Jane was baby-sitting <u>before</u> she went to the party.
3. I have to study <u>if</u> I want to pass a test.
4. I can eat <u>whenever</u> I am hungry.

EXERCISE 2

Several different names have been given to the group of function words you have found. We prefer the name "subordinators," although the term is not always used by linguists. Can you see any similarities between the patterning of these words and the patterning of conjunctions?
For every conjunction in the sentences below, try to substitute a subordinator.

1. John went to school and Mary stayed at home.
2. Susan and her mother ate ice cream cones.
3. The seal clapped his flippers and barked for a fish.
4. The dog ate his supper but the kitten played with her mouse.
5. The woman stormed out the door and down the street.

Write in your notebook a description of the differences between the patterning of subordinators and conjunctions.

In the cases where subordinators and conjunctions pattern alike some method is required to distinguish between them. Before doing the next exercise, try to imagine some test that would help you to tell them apart.

EXERCISE 3

Study the following sentences carefully:

1. John did his homework while he waited for the bus.
2. While he waited for the bus, John did his homework.
3. We lost the game because our best player was sick.
4. Because our best player was sick, we lost the game.
5. Mary went straight home after she left the dance.
6. After she left the dance, Mary went straight home.
7. The clock struck twelve and the lights went out.
8 And the lights went out, the clock struck twelve.

Write a sentence explaining how you can test to determine whether a word is a subordinator or a conjunction.

EXERCISE 4

In the last three exercises, you were dealing with what linguists call "clauses." More specifically, you dealt with two kinds of clauses—independent clauses and dependent clauses. Your task in doing this exercise is two-fold: (1) to describe what a clause is, and (2) to state the difference between an independent and dependent clause.

The following structures are *independent* clauses.

1. John did his homework
2. We lost the game
3. He waited for the bus
4. Our best player was sick
5. Mary went straight home

The following structures are *dependent* clauses.

1. While John did his homework
2. Because we lost the game
3. After we waited for the bus
4. Unless our best player was sick
5. Whenever Mary went straight home

Can you answer the following questions?

1. Is an "independent clause" another name for structures you have already studied?
2. What is the difference between an independent and dependent clause?
3. Can you guess why the names "independent" and "dependent" clauses are used?

Write your answers carefully in your notebook.

A dependent clause is formed by a subordinator and a basic sentence pattern. A sentence can be expanded through the use of a dependent clause, just as it can be through the use of a phrase. If you recall what you learned about phrases, you will probably want to know if dependent clauses can pattern in place of particular kinds of words. Look back at the examples of dependent clauses you worked with in Exercise 3 and try to make an "educated guess."

Can dependent clauses be substituted for single words, and vice versa? If so, what kinds of words?

Write down your guess; then work on the next exercise to test your idea.

EXERCISE 5

Identify the dependent clauses in the sentences below. Test words from each of the four form-classes to see whether or not they can pattern in place of the dependent clause.

1. I missed my breakfast because I overslept.
2. Jim ran down the hall whenever the teachers were not looking.
3. The rocket circled the earth twice before it reentered the atmosphere.
4. While I am visiting my grandparents, I can drive their car.
5. Will you pay me five dollars if I mow the lawn?

Was your guess correct?

If not, rewrite your statement so that it will accurately describe the facts.

205

EXPLORATION OF EXPANSIONS

We have discussed only one kind of subordinator. There is
another group of words which also introduces dependent
clauses. This kind of clause patterns somewhat differently
from the type with which we have just been working.

In each sentence below the dependent clause is underlined.
The first word of each clause is a subordinator. Study the
sentences; then, answer the questions which follow.

1. Madame Curie was the woman who discovered radium.
2. The dog that bit him is a German shepherd.
3. I know a girl who is named Esmeralda.
4. The man whose wallet was lost couldn't pay
   his check.
5. The coach, who was disappointed over the
   team's loss, walked slowly to the locker room.
6. I know a secret which cannot be told.
7. The money which I gave you belongs to my
   father.

Questions to answer:

1. If you omit the subordinator in each dependent
   clause above, does the rest of the clause form a
   complete sentence pattern?
2. Can phrases be substituted for any of the clauses?
   Give examples.
3. Can single words be substituted for any of the
   clauses? Give examples.
4. What type of word does each clause follow?

5. What similarities do you see between these dependent clauses and the dependent clauses we discussed earlier?
6. What differences do you see?
7. Can you substitute a conjunction for any of the subordinators above?
8. Do you want to distinguish between the two groups of clauses in any way? If so, what method do you suggest?

EXERCISE 7

Expand each of the following sentences by substituting, first a phrase, then a clause, for the underlined word. The phrase or clause should have the same structural relationship to the sentence that the underlined word has.

Example: The sentence: Birds fly <u>easily.</u>

Phrase expansion: Birds fly by instinct.

Clause expansion: Birds fly because they have wings.

1. Some <u>colonial</u> men wore beards.
2. This dog is a <u>superior</u> hunter.
3. Our team won <u>overwhelmingly</u>.
4. My brother <u>greedily</u> gobbled his food.
5. The <u>final</u> experiment failed.
6. The experiment failed <u>completely</u>.
7. <u>Quickly</u> the <u>young</u> woman left.

What further statements can you make about dependent clauses after completing the above exercise?

What have you discovered about the two different types of dependent clauses?

What have you discovered about the positions of dependent clauses in relation to other words in the sentence?

CHAPTER 24

Contracting expanded structures

You have had quite a bit of practice in expanding sentences. Expansion is an important aid to writing, and as you become more adept at expanding sentences your writing is likely to improve.

Contraction of sentences is also important, however. In contracting a sentence, we remove structures like phrases and clauses. We can even remove the Class III and the Class IV words and any intensifiers which are used with them.

Contracting a sentence may help you in your reading. If you are able to see the basic structure of the sentence, without modifiers, you may more quickly grasp the meaning of long and complicated sentences. Often, when you "proofread," you can improve your own ambiguous sentences by using contraction.

EXERCISE 1

Contract each sentence which follows, but do so in stages. First, remove any dependent clauses, and rewrite the sentence. Then remove any phrases, and rewrite the sentence. Then remove any other modifiers, and rewrite the sentence. Your final sentence should show the basic pattern around which the sentence was built.

Example:	Sentence:	John, who is a good friend of mine, saw a very exciting ball game in Centerport yesterday.
	With dependent clauses removed:	John saw a very exciting game in Centerport yesterday.
	With phrases removed:	John saw a very exciting ball game yesterday.
	With other modifiers removed:	John saw a game.

Basic sentence pattern: 1 2 d 1.

1. It was a sunny day in early May.
2. All fifteen members of the Beta Upsilon sorority were seated around the table that they laughingly called their "study" table.
3. No one in the Beta Upsilon sorority ever did school work at the table, but the girls frequently met there and discussed their social problems.
4. At present the topic of discussion was one Ronald Johnson, who had earned his position of importance by the simple method of breaking a date with the club's president.
5. Although the girls had liked Ronald until this incident, they were now determined that he must learn a lesson.
6. It was a dark and stormy night.

7. The wind that whistled through the trees sent shivers down the spine of the frightened boy who hid in the shadow of the giant oak tree.
8. As he watched the street light swinging back and forth and noticed the changing patterns of shadow it created, he wondered again about his reason for being there.
9. Why had he insisted that he would take Jim's dare, when even Jim had admitted that it was too dangerous?
10. His own action was a mystery to him, and now he must solve an even greater mystery.

EXERCISE 2

Sentences are sometimes classified according to the number and kinds of clauses they contain. For example:

A sentence with one independent clause is called a *simple sentence.*

A sentence which contains two or more independent clauses is called a *compound sentence.*

A sentence which contains one independent clause and one or more dependent clauses is called a *complex sentence.*

Write five examples of each kind of sentence listed above.

Can you guess the name usually given to a sentence which contains two or more independent clauses and one or more dependent clauses?

Classify each sentence below as simple, compound, or complex. Indicate the basic sentence pattern of each independent clause.

1. The girls walked into the kitchen of the model home and looked out the window into the back yard.
2. Many people drive foreign cars, but most Americans own domestic models.
3. Before the men stopped working, they covered the well with boards.
4. The two boys dove into the water and raced across the river.
5. Any student who misses his bus will have to walk home.
6. The movie will begin at 2:00 P.M., and I will meet you at 1:45.
7. Will you please iron my shirt after you finish washing the dishes?

8. June bought some shoes at the store where her brother works, and got a discount.
9. Wobble that wibble before wingle welks the wiggity.
10. Many boopers flipped the dip who beegled by bugment.

EXERCISE 4

Construct sentences for the following patterns. Phrases are underlined, and dependent clauses are set off by parentheses. (s stands for subordinator.)

1. d 3 1 c d 1 a 4 2 <u>p d 1 p d 1</u>.
2. (s 1 2 1) 1 2 d 1 c 2 d 1.
3. 1 4 2 <u>p d 1</u> c d 1 4 2 <u>p d 1</u>.
4. d 3 1 <u>p d 1</u> a <u>2 p d 1</u> (s 1 2 1).
5. a 1 2 1 (s 1 2 i 3 <u>p 1</u>)?
6. d 1 (s 2 <u>p 1</u>) 2 d 1 p 1.

7. 2 d 1 4 c ı a 2 p d 1.
8. (s 1 2 4) d 1 2 4 d 1 p d 1 p ı?
9. 1 2 4 p d 3 1 c p d 3 1 c 1 2 d 1 p d 3 1.

PART VII

Further Explorations

CHAPTER 25

Independent language investigations

We hope this last chapter in the book will start you on your way to interesting language investigation and activity. If you read carefully our description of each of the "projects" we propose, you should find some which you would like to pursue. Or, perhaps you and your classmates prefer doing each of the projects together. In any case, we are sure that once you have assumed responsibility for working on a project, you will work vigorously and carefully, as any language scientist would.

Before we present our slate of language problems, we know you will be interested in reading the last communication the authors received from our friend, the learned Venutian. Actually, the message was in the form of a letter, and, so far as we can tell, it was addressed to you. Here it is.

"Dear Earth Boys and Girls,

"I have, for the time being, decided to remain on Venus, where I have obtained a teaching position at the Institute for Inter-planetary Studies. As you might have guessed, I have been assigned to the Primitive Planet Department. I will teach courses in Earth languages, specializing in the language which is spoken by more Earth people than any other—English. Believe me, I could use your help! Even though Venutians are much smarter than Earth people and even though I am a particularly smart Venutian, the English language is not at all easy for me to describe and analyze. If only I had one of you here with me, my teaching job would be simple. But there is no chance of any of you getting here for many, many years (Earth time), and I am afraid I must do without you for a week or two (Venus time).

"I have known all along that you have been reading my books and articles. To tell the truth, you were my most devoted readers. Venutians, for all of their advanced mentality, are frequently very harsh critics. Although I know you didn't believe everything I wrote, I think you enjoyed a great deal of it. I thank you for your interest.

"I have grown quite fond of all Earth people, but you were my particular favorites. Not only were you friendly and attentive, but you were the hardest working group of scholars I observed anywhere. Perhaps we will all meet again soon. If you cannot get your rockets to Venus, I will just have to make another visit to my 'favorite primitive planet.' Then I could write another book entitled, *The Return of the Inter-planetary Traveler.* Goodby. I hope you solve some of your important planetary problems.

"Cosmically yours,

The Venutian"

Project 1

We are sure you will all want to do this project. Write a letter to the Venutian. Tell him what you think of him, his observations, his scientific methods, his new job, his plan to return to Earth, and the possibility of Earth men going to Venus. You may also discuss any other idea you would like to communicate. You can address your letter to:

> Department of Primitive Planets
> Institute for Inter-planetary Studies
> Venus, Solar System

Project 2

Every science has its special terminology. Physicists talk of *atoms* and *particles*. Biologists talk of *chromosomes* and *cell nuclei*. Psychologists talk of *ego* and *anxiety*. During your work, you have had to use many special terms that are probably not familiar to most people. Your task in this project is to develop a dictionary of linguistic terms. You must first list, in alphabetical order, all of the terms you know. Your linguistics notebook will come in very handy here. Then you must explain each term as clearly as you can. Write your explanation in a manner such that a person who has not studied linguistics can understand it. You will probably need to include a great many examples or illustrations.

In order to get you started, we have listed below a few of the terms you have used in your work this year. The terms are not listed alphabetically, since we do not wish to do too much of *your* work.

Subject of a sentence	Intonation
Object	Prepositional Phrase
Form-class	Dialect
Determiner	Auxiliary
Tense	Function word

Project 3

Any good scientist will tell you that it is unwise for anyone to depend too much on one book or one point of view. We hope you have found *Discovering Your Language* worthwhile to read. But we would not want you to think that its authors are any wiser than a great many other authors of language books. Therefore, you ought to make some plans to read other books which deal with language.

You should first visit your school library. Consult with the librarian. Perhaps she can suggest several books on language that would be interesting for you to read. You should also visit the library in your neighborhood or a bookstore near your home. When you have done all this, you are to compile a list of books on language suitable for you and your classmates. Then, you are to read one or two of them. Finally, you are to report to the rest of the class on each book you have read. Perhaps you will discover that *Discovering Your Language* has misled you on some points. Perhaps something you have studied this year will be more clearly explained in another book. In any case, in presenting your report to the class, you should try to inform the class of what the book is about, and to explain why you would or would not recommend it to them.

Project 4

We have pointed out a great many times in this text that language is a form of behavior, similar in some respects to the way we dress or eat or play. For example, other people judge you by the way you dress. If you wear a black leather jacket and tight pants, some people might think you are a "hot rodder" and, perhaps, ill-mannered. Similarly, if you frequently use expressions like "I ain't got it," or "He don't know nothing," some people might think you have been badly educated or that you do not care much for education. Actually, such judgments are not very scientific. Some of the best mannered people we know like to wear black leather jackets. And some educated people say things like, "I ain't got it." But the fact remains that we live in a society in which people are judged by the way they speak and dress.

Your task in this project is to discover something about those expressions which are claimed to be an indication of ignorance or illiteracy. Your first step is to compile a list of words or expressions that are "suspect." You know some of them already: *Ain't, He don't, Joe and me gave it to him.* Your teacher is certain to know many others. After you have compiled your list, you must try to determine how different kinds of people feel toward each item. For example, you might construct a questionnaire which can be filled out by teachers, students, businessmen, policemen, etc. The questionnaire might begin in this way:

> We are trying to find out what your attitude is toward each one of the underlined expressions in the following sentences. Please put an "X" in the box that best represents your feeling.
>
> 1. I *ain't* going.
>
> ☐ Nothing is wrong with it. I use it myself.
> ☐ I do not use it myself, but it does not bother me.
>
> ☐ People who use the word *ain't* are probably not well educated.

223

☐   It shocks me. Every educated person should avoid using it.

When your questionnaires are completed, you should organize your data and present them to the class. Perhaps you will find that some of the "suspected" expressions are "not guilty." Your teacher and other teachers of English are more than likely to find your research extremely valuable.

Project 5

Project 4 was a study of "usage." This project is a study of "dialectic differences." English speech is different in different sections of the country. Your task is to discover some of these differences. Your first step is to exploit whatever information your classmates can give you. Perhaps one member of the class has lived in another section of the country. He or she might be able to tell you about different meanings and pronunciations of familiar words.

Your second step is to consult a good reference book. The school librarian can help you here. The group working on Project 3 (compiling a bibliography) can also give you some leads. Your third step is to listen carefully whenever you are watching television or are at the movies or are listening to the radio. You are almost certain to hear people using varied pronunciations and expressions that will reflect the fact that they come from differing parts of the country.

224

After you have collected your data, you must organize them. Then, you must present your results to the class in as clear and as interesting a manner as possible.

Project 6

At one time, writers of English did not use punctuation. In fact, there was a time when words were not even separated from each other by a space. A line in a book would have looked something like this:

INTHISPROJECTYOUWILLSTUDYPUNCTUATION

That was many years ago. For hundreds of years now, writers, editors, and printers have worked to develop a system of punctuation that would be clear and consistent. Your task in this project is to discover as much about our punctuation system as possible. For example, you can choose to investigate the history of punctuation. Or, after listing all of the punctuation marks you can discover— periods, semi-colons, question marks, etc.—you can then explain what each is for and provide an example of how each is used. Your final report to the class ought to be both fascinating and informative.

Project 7

You have had a great deal of experience in guided ob- servations of the structure of English. Many of you are now able to make some independent observations. To begin with, take a simply written book. The *Let's Read!* books are excellent for this project, if they are available in your school. Select one or two pages at random and classify all the words which are familiar to you. This will help you to isolate unfamiliar structures.

Once you have identified some unfamiliar structure, use the procedures you have learned to determine its identifying characteristics. It will be your privilege to name the structure you have discovered.

When your investigation is complete, report your results to your classmates. Make sure that you have plenty of evidence to support your conclusions.

Project 8

This project will enable you to apply your knowledge of English structure to the field of literature. It is a difficult assignment, but you may find it very exciting.

Choose a well-known author with whom you are familiar. Charles Dickens, Edgar Allan Poe, Washington Irving, Guy de Maupassant, and Jules Verne are good examples of authors you might use. Classify the words in the introductory paragraphs of a story by this author. Then write your own story, following the same sentence patterns. The subject of your story will be original, but you will be writing in the "style" of the author you have chosen.

Project 9

Most scientists will tell you that the most difficult part of their work is finding useful questions to ask. The greatest scientists have been, almost without exception, those who have phrased questions that no one had asked before. Therefore, this project is the most difficult of all for you to do. It requires you to invent your own project! In other words, you must think of some question which is both worth answering and capable of being answered. Then, you must proceed to do whatever work is required in order to find the answer to your question. Good luck!

Project 10

This project will give you an opportunity to do something that a great many linguists have wished they could do: You can invent your own grammar!

The first step you ought to take is to review some of the important facts about the grammar of English: its word order, its inflections and suffixes, its form-classes, its function words, its basic sentence patterns, its methods of expansion and contraction. Then, you should try to invent a grammar that is as different from the grammar of English as it can possibly be. For example, perhaps you can invent a grammar in which the subject of a sentence always comes after a Class II word, and the object always comes before. Thus, the sentence "The man bit the dog," in *your* grammar, would mean that the man was attacked and the dog was the attacker. Or, perhaps you can invent a grammar which does not have subjects of sentences at all, or one in which the word order has no significance. You are free to imagine any kind of grammar you wish. The only condition you must meet is this: *You must be able to explain to your classmates how your grammar works.* That is, you should be able to explain what are its basic patterns, how these patterns can be expanded, and how the grammar may be analyzed. Who knows? Your grammar may be extremely useful for communicating with creatures from outer space . . . if there are any creatures in outer space!

DE BEATLES BAS HERE